AFTER SHOCKS

Stand Strong!

JEFF KINLEY

[signature]
PS 46:1-3

HARVEST PROPHECY
AN IMPRINT OF HARVEST HOUSE PUBLISHERS

D0863398

Published in association with William K. Jensen Literary Agency, 119 Bampton Court, Eugene, Oregon 97404

Cover design by Bryce Williamson

Cover photo © Varunyu, inkoly, StudioM1/ Gettyimages

Interior design by Greg Longbons

For bulk, special sales, or ministry purchases, please call 1-800-547-8979. Email: Customerservice@hhpbooks.com

Aftershocks

Copyright © 2021 by Jeff Kinley
Published by Harvest House Publishers
Eugene, Oregon 97408
www.harvesthousepublishers.com

ISBN 978-0-7369-8410-2 (pbk.)
ISBN 978-0-7369-8411-9 (eBook)

Library of Congress Cataloging-in-Publication Data

Names: Kinley, Jeff, author.
Title: Aftershocks : Christians entering a new era of global crisis / Jeff Kinley.
Description: Eugene, Oregon : Harvest House Publishers, 2021. | Includes
  bibliographical references.
Identifiers: LCCN 2020047886 (print) | LCCN 2020047887 (ebook) | ISBN
  9780736984102 (pbk) | ISBN 9780736984119 (ebook)
Subjects: LCSH: End of the world. | Church and the world. |
  Globalization—Religious aspects—Christianity.
Classification: LCC BT877 .K56 2021 (print) | LCC BT877 (ebook) | DDC
  236—dc23
LC record available at https://lccn.loc.gov/2020047886
LC ebook record available at https://lccn.loc.gov/2020047887

Printed in the United States of America

21 22 23 24 25 26 27 28 29 / BP / 10 9 8 7 6 5 4 3 2

Dedicated to my fellow watchers and discerners,
and all those who long to hear "the last trumpet."

1 Corinthians 15:51-52

CONTENTS

Restless Planet 7

1. The Great Revealer 11

2. Globalism at the Gates 27

3. Caesar and God 43

4. Technology and Satan's Superman 65

5. The End-Times Economic Collapse 81

6. Israel and the Rise of Antisemitism 97

7. Times of the Signs 117

8. The Coming Super Crisis 139

9. Be Still and Know That I Am God 161

10. Our Finest Hour 179

Notes 196

RESTLESS PLANET

Duane Carriker was finishing up his workday in the little Prince William Sound port city of Valdez, Alaska. Having moved there a few years earlier with his wife, Bonnie, and their two small children, Duane had found work on the docks as a longshoreman. But driving a forklift wasn't his real passion. Ministry was. Duane's calling was to preach the gospel and lead others to Jesus. And he no doubt looked forward to this upcoming weekend, as he would be ringing the church bell at Valdez Gospel Chapel, calling the area townspeople to Good Friday worship. It was March 27, 1964. Tragically, that Friday proved to be anything but good for Duane, as by dinnertime, the 34-year-old pastor would be dead.

At 5:36 p.m., a colossal earthquake rocked the Alaskan coast. Registering a massive 9.2 on the Richter scale, it would prove to be the most powerful earthquake in US history.[1] So strong was the colossal quake that it swayed Seattle's Space Needle 1,200 miles to the south. And its ripple effects disrupted rivers and lakes as far away as Texas and Louisiana.[2]

Back in Valdez, telephone poles toppled and snapped like toothpicks. Sewer lines ruptured, railroad tracks splintered, and roads split in half. Whole forests suddenly plunged below sea level as the coastline soil liquified and sank. There were hundreds of landslides.[3]

And then came the tsunamis.

Footage shot by crew aboard a ship docked in Valdez documents the moment bay waters abruptly receded, nearly draining the bay dry. The ship then rapidly began sinking into a giant crevice on the ocean floor as a 70-foot high wall of water raced toward the shoreline. This just four minutes following the initial quake. The dock on which Carriker was standing simply disappeared into the dark abyss below. There was no time to escape and nowhere to run. His body was never found.

Near the Valdez dock, Union oil tanks exploded and burned for nearly two weeks, producing an apocalyptic scene of devastation. In nearby Shoup Bay, a tsunami measuring more than 200 feet high hit land, as did others in Oregon and California. Most of the more than 130 people who perished did so as a result of the tsunamis.

On the day of the earthquake, there were 11 recorded aftershocks, each of them measuring a magnitude of at least 6.0. Smaller aftershocks continued for *more than a year*.

But this is not a book about earthquakes. It's not about tectonic plates grinding together and wreaking havoc on land or at sea. It's not about Richter scales and ruined cities. Instead, it's about something much worse. And more serious.

Aftershocks is about God's prophetic plan for the ages, and your part in it.

It's no secret that recent national and global events have dramatically altered the moral, economic, and geopolitical landscapes of planet Earth. But in doing so, they have also triggered a series of aftershocks, some being immediate and strong, while others linger on the horizon, as if waiting for their cue to bring more seismic upheaval to humanity.

Aftershocks will supply you with critical intel concerning how life will likely change for you, your family, community, culture, and church in the months and years ahead. This book will help you develop biblical discernment, enabling you to X-ray current events and know how to respond in wisdom. You'll learn how recent cultural convulsions on this restless planet play into heaven's prophetic plan for Earth and its inhabitants. It will give you a "God's-eye view" of what's happening.

Undeniably, we are in a prophetic season of global change, and it is imperative for us as Christians to comprehend the perilous times in which we live, to know what we believe, and to live courageously going forward.

Aftershocks unveils the raw reality of these last days while simultaneously inspiring you with hope—a hope that vaccinates you against the viral ignorance, naivety, and anxiety that plague so many today.

Jesus told His disciples, "We must work the works of Him who sent Me as long as it is day; night is coming when no man can work. While I am in the world, I am the Light of the world" (John 9:4).

While humanity desperately attempts to steady itself during tumultuous times, we Christians find ourselves standing on the precipice of a historic moment, facing a once-in-a-millennium opportunity. We can still make a difference in our world. But it has to be now—while it is still "day" for us. Time is running out. There are no do-overs in this brief life. We get one shot, and this is *our* appointment with destiny. Miss this opportunity, and we may be remembered in heaven's history books as the most undiscerning and ineffective generation of believers.

But, if we wake up, wise up, and rise up, then at some point in the future, perhaps at the *bema* judgment seat of Christ or in the coming millennial kingdom, Jesus Christ will proudly say of us, "This, My bride, was your *finest hour*!"

JEFF KINLEY

Chapter 1

THE GREAT REVEALER

In the well-known European folktale *Chicken Little*, the main character is walking along one day, minding his own business, when an acorn unexpectedly falls on his head. Looking up and seeing nothing above him, Chicken Little falsely assumes that the sky must be collapsing. This perceived reality soon becomes his battle cry: "The sky is falling! The sky is falling!" Like a poultry version of Paul Revere, Chicken Little embarks on a mission to bring this urgent news to the king, heralding his message of doom wherever he goes. Along the way, he encounters various other farmyard animals, stirring them all into a similar frenzied fear. Finally, the animals encounter Foxy Loxy, who invites them one by one into his den, where presumably, he eats them. As it turns out, the sky wasn't falling after all.

The story of Chicken Little has often been cited, and sometimes appropriately so, in an effort to debunk and discredit the crazed rants of Christian "doomsday preachers." Their fearmongering typically includes apocalyptic speculations and predictions of imminent judgment and devastation. Sadly, these exaggerations end up producing more paranoia and anxiety than they do actual preparation for the end of days.

Contamination, Chaos, and Crime

Like the boy who cried "Wolf!," Chicken Little is a classic laughingstock. But tragically, those who proclaim and teach Bible prophecy are often associated with these fictitious literary characters. And why not? For despite centuries of waiting for the Lord's return, Jesus has, in fact, not returned…at least not yet. This has given rise to a culture that regularly mocks Scripture's prophetic predictions concerning the Lord's coming in the last days. However, this too was prophesied. Writing to first-century believers scattered and suffering all across Asia Minor, Peter wrote,

> Know this first of all, that in the last days mockers will come with their mocking, following after their own lusts, and saying, "Where is the promise of His coming? For ever since the fathers fell asleep, all continues just as it was from the beginning of creation" (2 Peter 3:3-4).

The scoffers' argument here is based upon a presupposition that assumes there are no forces outside of nature and science that can alter the created order. To them, the world is a closed system, one in which no supposed "God" can enter. Therefore, it is impossible to penetrate time and space in order to alter basic reality here. They also conclude that because no global judgment such as predicted by Scripture has ever happened in the past, it therefore cannot happen in the future.

However, Peter counters this claim by stating that these mockers willfully ignore the authenticity and credibility of God's Word concerning *past* prophetic events, specifically citing the judgment of

Noah's flood. He adds that the present heavens and Earth are being preserved by God's powerful Word and "are reserved for fire, kept for the day of judgment and destruction of ungodly men" (3:5-7).

Jude, the half-brother of Jesus, echoes this truth:

> You, beloved, ought to remember the words that were spoken beforehand by the apostles of our Lord Jesus Christ, that they were saying to you, "In the last time there will be mockers, following after their own ungodly lusts." These are the ones who cause divisions, worldly-minded, devoid of the spirit (Jude 17-19).

Are we as Christians genuinely delusional and misguided, like Chicken Little? When we point others to Scripture's prophecies in the midst of chaotic, cataclysmic times of global disturbance, are we really the crazy ones here? Or is it possible that those mockers and scoffers Peter wrote about are simply choosing to dismiss the evidence staring them in the face?

Enter the 2020 COVID-19 pandemic, an outbreak that blindsided planet Earth, catching us flatfooted and unprepared. What began in a laboratory in Wuhan, China, quickly spread like wildfire across the entire globe in just a matter of weeks.[1] And as it gained momentum, a follow-up pandemic of panic spread as well, sending entire countries into lockdown mode. Economies ground to a screeching halt. Citizens were forced to retreat into their homes. Businesses were forcibly shut down. Corporations furloughed employees. Manufacturers shut off machines, shutting down production. Schools, colleges, and universities canceled classes for the rest of the year, sending them scrambling to adopt remote-learning methods. Churches closed their doors, transitioning to online services. Some pastors even printed pictures of their congregation, taping them to chairs and pews while preaching to an empty building.

Streets were empty and silent. Shops were closed. Times Square echoed with emptiness, and Main Street America resembled a giant ghost town.

Grocery shelves were suddenly bare as frantic shoppers desperately stockpiled everything from toilet paper to hand sanitizer. Air travel was grounded, with airports packed with parked planes, while the trucking industry became strangled by the choking grip of this virus epidemic. Overnight, hospital personnel became the new heroes of the age. Makeshift medical testing facilities were set up. Temporary hospital facilities were hastily assembled in warehouses and even parking garages, anticipating the tens of thousands of cases of COVID-19 that were predicted. And the medical community braced itself, as if anticipating an unavoidable, approaching tsunami.

New phrases and concepts were injected into our vocabulary as *social distancing* and *sheltering in place* became the vernacular. Breathing masks became as common as cell phones, though the demand for them made them scarce early on. Signs with the number *6* lined streets, reminding people to keep a distance of six feet from others to help prevent the spread of the disease.

But there were also serious concerns about the *mental* health of citizens worldwide as billions were virtually banned from outside contact for weeks on end.

And then all hell broke loose.

In Minneapolis, a white police officer arrested a black man—George Floyd—following his attempt to pass a counterfeit $20 bill. In his body at the time were traces of morphine, fentanyl, cannabis, and methamphetamine. A former convict multiple times, he had also tested positive for the coronavirus.[2] But as it turned out, none of that really mattered as the arresting officer foolishly kept his knee on the man's neck for some eight minutes, contributing to his death.

Despite Floyd's past offenses or crime that day, none of them warranted being killed. It was a senseless tragedy at the worst of times.

And with growing accusations of racism and systemic police brutality against the black community already rumbling beneath the surface, a seismic eruption ensued as a firestorm of violent retribution was ignited all across America. Fueled and funded even further by radical neo-Marxist groups, American cities were subsequently set ablaze, causing a chain reaction of rampant looting, vandalism, violent assaults, and even murders following in its wake. Downtown areas in Minneapolis, Portland, Seattle, Atlanta, Chicago, and Pittsburgh saw violent protests, with a portion of Seattle's downtown overtaken by mob rule for weeks. All of this was sheer unbridled madness on parade.

Notwithstanding some actual peaceful protests, civility and justice stood silently by as unhinged and angry rioters took to America's streets to flesh out their vengeance and evil desires. Shop owners of all races were brutally assaulted and even killed. Police officers were also murdered.[3] As it turned out, the color of one's skin mattered little to these crazed rioters, as black-owned businesses were also looted, despite pleas for peace.[4] It soon became clear that their justification for rampant violence was not retribution for one man's death, or even payback for perceived systemic racism. Rather, it was an excuse to simply unleash lawlessness and anarchy—to steal, kill, and destroy, which mirrors the enemy's own objectives against humanity (John 10:10).

The Big Reveal

All this makes us wonder how people today could stoop to such vile, uncontrollable behavior. How has society gotten to this point? And what does it all mean? Biblically, this vitriolic and uncontrollable lust for domination does have a precedent. The spirit fueling these actions is reminiscent of that present in the godless, sin-fueled mob appearing at Lot's door in Genesis 19. The reprobate men of Sodom had gathered to demand the release of his two angel visitors. But for what purpose? They wanted to gang-rape them (verses 4-5). Lot, having absorbed some of his culture's values, and under the illusion that he could actually reason with this angry homosexual horde, proposed an incredulous compromise, offering them his two daughters instead!

But like hungry sharks, the maniacal mob had already smelled blood and were hell-bent on devouring their prey. They accused Lot of judging them (and by doing so, committed the same offense!), vowing to rape or kill him as well after finishing with his angelic guests.

However, God's messengers had had enough. Forcefully pulling Lot inside, they struck the entire riotous gang with blindness. But even this did not deter them. Scripture records that "they wearied themselves trying to find the doorway" (verse 11).

A similar spirit of "group sin" is alive today and is part of what Paul prophesied would occur in the end times:

> Realize this, that in the last days difficult times will come. For men will be lovers of self, lovers of money, boastful, arrogant, revilers, disobedient to parents, ungrateful, unholy, unloving, irreconcilable, malicious gossips, without self-control, brutal, haters of good, treacherous, reckless, conceited, lovers of pleasure rather than lovers of God, holding to a form of godliness, although they have denied its power; Avoid such men as these…evil men and impostors will proceed from bad to worse, deceiving and being deceived (2 Timothy 3:1-5, 13).

Roughly 30 years before Paul wrote those words, Jesus was asked by His disciples, "What will be the sign of Your coming, and of the end of the age?" (Matthew 24:3). The Lord responded by painting a verbal portrait of the tribulation period (Matthew 24:3–25:46). He described the character of those days, explaining that "because lawlessness is increased, most people's love will grow cold" (24:12). John adds that during this future seven-year period, rampant evil and a total disregard for moral and civil law will reign supreme (Revelation 9:20-21).

We are currently ramping up to that era. Ours is an age where sin has become rampant, accepted, and even applauded in mainstream culture. Just as in the days of Noah (Matthew 24:37), this unchecked disdain for moral law will be accompanied by perverse passions and desires, which is precisely what Paul spelled out for us in his letter to the believers in Rome. He depicted a culture where people are

> filled with all unrighteousness, wickedness, greed, evil; full of envy, murder, strife, deceit, malice; they are gossips, slanderers, haters of God, insolent, arrogant, boastful, inventors of evil, disobedient to parents, without understanding, untrustworthy, unloving, unmerciful; and although they know the ordinance of God, that those who practice such things are worthy of death, they not only do the same, but also give hearty approval to those who practice them (Romans 1:29-32).

These words eerily and accurately describe the day we live in now. Such beliefs and behavior are indicative of a person, culture, people group, or nation that has suffered abandonment by God, having been delivered over to a depraved mind (Romans 1:28). We live in an evil age where passion rules over reason. Where truth is no longer objective, but relative and personal. Where self-love is considered the height of virtue. A culture that allows evil to be incubated. And those who succumb to such decadence are thus robbed of experiencing real love, evidenced by the fact that they show no mercy to those who would dare question them, disagree, or offer rational solutions to the ills they purportedly oppose. Unfazed, they run headlong into wickedness, practicing these evils and heartily approving, financing, and celebrating those who participate in them. They personify these ancient words of Isaiah:

> Woe to those who call evil good, and good evil;
> Who substitute darkness for light and light for darkness;
> Who substitute bitter for sweet and sweet for bitter!
> Woe to those who are wise in their own eyes
>> And clever in their own sight!
> Woe to those who are heroes and drinking wine
>> And valiant men in mixing strong drink,
> Who declare the wicked innocent for a bribe,
>> And take away the rights of the ones who are in the right!
>> (Isaiah 5:20-23).

And God declares that not a single one of them will be able to justify themselves on that day when they stand before heaven's Great White Throne (Romans 1:20, 32; Revelation 20:11-15). As a consequence of their stubborn rejection of God's existence, an inward suppression of His moral law, and a stubborn, pride-filled defiance of His lordship, their minds have become "darkened," literally losing their ability to think rationally (Romans 1:21).

Regrettably, despite calls for peace from all sides, it is unlikely the wounds and scars from America's recent civil unrest and violence will ever fully heal. The year 2020 (a number that has become synonymous with calamity and doom, and which has all but outpaced the number 13 as being "unlucky") may be remembered as a watershed year of disease, death, destruction, and despair.

What Lies Beneath

But where does all this recent fear, hatred, and lawlessness come from? Was all this really caused by a microscopic virus and the unjustified death of a black man? Or could a much deeper seismic fault be to blame?

For nine years, our family enjoyed the company of a loving Golden Retriever named Lucy. Muscular and strong, this dog was the most spirited animal we had ever owned. She could gallop across our property like a thoroughbred. Lucy was energetic and full of life, the epitome of a family pet. But immediately prior to leaving for a week-long speaking engagement, my wife noticed that after she threw a ball to Lucy, the dog walked back to her instead of running like she normally would. Though that seemed a bit odd, we didn't think much of it.

Upon returning a week later, our house sitter informed us that Lucy had stopped eating, which was out of character for a dog with such a voracious appetite. A trip to the veterinarian revealed that Lucy was full of tumors and had little time left to live. We learned that dogs like her typically conceal their diseases until it's too late for anything to be done. As it turns out, Lucy's symptoms were the culmination of a sickness that had been brewing inside her for many years.

People and cultures can be like that too.

Pandemics, injustices, godless political leadership, violence, global unrest—none of these current phenomena *caused* the internal crisis billions are feeling worldwide. To the contrary, the events of recent days have merely pulled back the curtain, exposing the true character of many across our nation and around the planet. The sin virus we see exploding all around us has been present all along—it's just that some of it remained concealed until now.

Jesus revealed this discerning spiritual principle in Mark 7:14-23:

> Listen to Me, all of you, and understand: there is nothing outside the man which can defile him if it goes into him; but the things which proceed out of the man are what defile the man.
>
> When he had left the crowd and entered the house, His disciples questioned Him about the parable. And He said to them, "Are you so lacking in understanding also? Do you not understand that whatever goes into the man from outside cannot defile him, because it does not go into his heart, but into his stomach, and is eliminated?" (Thus, He declared all foods clean.) And He was saying, "That which proceeds out of the man, that is what defiles the man. For from within, out of the heart of men, proceed the evil thoughts, fornications, thefts, murders, adulteries, deeds of coveting and wickedness, as well as deceit, sensuality, envy, slander, pride and foolishness. All these evil things proceed from within and defile the man.

The essence of Christ's teaching here is that sin originates not "out there" in the world or because of external calamity or crisis, but rather from within people's wicked hearts.

Six hundred years earlier, the prophet Jeremiah wrote, "The heart is more deceitful than all else and is desperately sick; who can understand it?" (Jeremiah 17:9). The apostle Paul, quoting the psalmist, confirmed this principle that our hearts are the birthplace and breeding ground of sinful thoughts, words, and actions:

> As it is written,
> There is none righteous, not even one;
>> There is none who understands,
>> There is none who seeks for God;
> All have turned aside, together they have become useless;

There is none who does good,
>   There is not even one.
Their throat is an open grave,
>   With their tongues they keep deceiving,
The poison of asps is under their lips;
>   Whose mouth is full of cursing and bitterness;
Their feet are swift to shed blood,
>   Destruction and misery are in their paths,
And the path of peace they have not known.
>   There is no fear of God before their eyes (Romans 3:10-18).

Sound familiar? Those brutally forthright words provide us with a biblically informed look at today's world.

In that same letter to the Christians at Rome, Paul even describes himself this way: "I know that nothing good dwells in me, that is, in my flesh" (7:18).

Strangely, though sin inherently resides within us all, we still somehow manage to blame others while simultaneously portraying *ourselves* as victims. We see it in the so-called social justice culture, where personal responsibility is rejected and replaced with violence and vengeance. We see it in the LGBTQ subculture, where the justification for certain feelings, identities, and lifestyles are summed up by saying, "God made me this way." More generally applied, all us fallen humans are masters at manufacturing mental realities that absolve us of being held responsible for our sin or our immoral lifestyles.

The Birthplace of Blame

Lest we are tempted to think recent developments are confined to current racial or moral issues, all we need to do is to rewind back to the Bible's inaugural book. In Genesis, we see the very first couple and the very first human sin. Following their disobedience to God in the garden, the Creator confronted mankind's original parents.

> They heard the sound of the LORD God walking in the garden in the [cool of the day, and the man and his wife hid themselves from the presence of the LORD God among the trees of the garden. Then the LORD God called to the man, and said to him, "Where are you?" He said, "I heard the sound of You in the garden, and I was afraid because I was naked; so, I hid myself." And He said, "Who told you that you were naked? Have you eaten from the tree of which I commanded you not to eat?" The man said, "The woman whom You gave to be with me, she gave me from the tree, and I ate." Then the LORD God said to the woman, "What is this you have done?" And the woman said, "The serpent deceived me, and I ate" (3:8-13).

Note that Adam immediately blamed his new wife and managed to fault God as well. It's as if he had said, "Hey, I innocently took a nap as a single man and somehow woke up married. I was just minding my own business, naming the animals, and next thing I know, *You* married me to this woman. It's You and her who are to blame for this."

Then the woman, following her husband's example, plays the blame game as well, claiming her sin was really the serpent's fault.

And thus, victimhood mentality was born.

But why? Why do we humans inherently run from responsibility and respond this way? Why is it rarely, if ever, *our* fault? Here again, God's Word gives us the answer. Though you or I may never have looted, rioted, or killed anyone, we still carry the same sin virus as do those who practice such things. The sin nature within us is like a stubborn king who refuses to surrender his throne to a rival ruler. Our fleshly rule over us began at birth, and all through our lives, its intricate root system deep within us affects every part of us. We hear about humans being totally depraved, but that doesn't mean each of us is as evil as we *could* be. Rather, it's that sin, self-centeredness, and self-preservation are our default mode. Sin's influence extends to every part of us, deeply influencing our mind, body, and soul.

Jesus knew this, and it's why He incorporated a "death sentence to self" in the requirements for being His disciple:

> If anyone comes to Me, and does not hate his own father and mother and wife and children and brothers and sisters, yes, and even his own life, he cannot be My disciple. Whoever does not carry his own cross and come after Me cannot be My disciple. For which one of you, when he wants to build a tower, does not first sit down and calculate the cost to see if he has enough to complete it? Otherwise, when he has laid a foundation and is not able to finish, all who observe it begin to ridicule him, saying, "This man began to build and was not able to finish." Or what king, when he sets out to meet another king in battle, will not first sit down and consider whether he is strong enough with ten thousand men to encounter the one coming against him with twenty thousand? Or else, while the other is still far away, he sends a delegation and asks for terms of peace. So then, none of you can be My disciple who does not give up all his own possessions.
>
> Therefore, salt is good; but if even salt has become tasteless, with what will it be seasoned? It is useless either for the soil or for the manure pile; it is thrown out. He who has ears to hear, let him hear (Luke 14:26-35).

"Count the cost before deciding to follow Me," Jesus says, "for if you do follow, I will demand total allegiance above all other loves, even the love of self and your very life. I will come and conquer your self-will like a king with a great army. So, make peace, lay down your weapons, and surrender all to Me."

In short, Jesus is a colossal threat to self. When He is Lord, self is not. When He is our sovereign King, by definition, that means we have been officially dethroned. And *this* is precisely why we resist taking responsibility for our sins and actions. To do so would be to surrender the pride of self that has established such a long-held stronghold in our lives. Admitting sin is a part of dying to self.

So, when the "quake of 2020" hit, rather than being the culprit causing our panic, despair, anger, and chaos, it simply cast a powerful searchlight onto humanity's heart, revealing a bondage to sin and self.

In short, adversity is the great revealer, whether it applies to a person, a nation, or a civilization. Crises uncover our true identity, exposing what was there all along.

Crises also reveal how fragile we are.

They demonstrate how easily we cower in fear and anxiety.

They divulge the hidden side of us.

They make dormant sins, biases, and hatred public.

They uncover how selfish and godless our hearts are.

And they show us just how rapidly the entire world can change. Just. Like. That.

Yes, these ongoing crises have taught us something about ourselves. About what lies deep within the soul.

> Good people can make laws and seek to bring "positive change" in culture, but godly people seek to alter *destinies*.

Sandcastles or Solid Rock?

In such perilous and uncertain days, Jesus' words become even more relevant and needed:

> Everyone who hears these words of Mine and acts on them, may be compared to a wise man who built his house on the rock. And the rain fell, and the floods came, and the winds blew and slammed against that house; and yet it did not fall, for it had been founded on the rock. Everyone who hears these words of Mine and does not act on them, will be like a foolish man who built his house on the sand. The rain fell, and the floods came, and the winds blew and slammed against that house; and it fell—and great was its fall (Matthew 7:24-27).

The application is simple:

1. Hear what Christ says.
2. Act upon His words.

That's what the rest of this book is about—listening to God's prophetic insights concerning the world in which we live, where it's going, and *why*. And what we can do about it.

Admittedly, it would be easier to simply withdraw into the safety of our Christian subculture and simply ride out the storm until Jesus comes. But He did not leave us that option. Ours is a higher calling. We are not only sheep who follow the Shepherd, but also warriors who march under the command of the Conquering King. Good people can make laws and seek to bring "positive change" in culture, but godly people seek to alter *destinies*. One is temporal, while the other is eternal and immeasurably more important. Christ specifically called us to "make disciples," which means engaging culture with news greater than peace, reconciliation, or justice. Ours is the message of salvation, out of which all other virtues flow.

But for this sort of spiritual change to come, we must first choose to reject victimhood, refuse to play the blame game, and accept personal responsibility concerning Christ's words. And we do this by building our hearts and homes upon the solid Rock. This means asking, "Is Jesus the center of my heart? Is He reigning over self?" If not, then pause right now and give Him His deserved access to that throne.

Second, share the simple truths of salvation with someone else, perhaps even beginning with your own story. After all, isn't this how sinners like you and I were saved? Someone listened, and obeyed, sharing the gospel that led to our salvation. And what has been done for us, we must also do for others. Don't worry about changing the whole world—just focus on those whom God has placed in your life.

And third, we cannot afford to shrink back or cower in fear as we face more dark days ahead. Instead, we are called to confidently move forward into that darkness, knowing that not even the gates of hell and death will prevail against us (Matthew 16:18). Your confidence is in Christ Himself. Never forget that, my friend.

With that in mind, what sort of aftershocks can we expect, both in the short and long term, should Jesus delay His return for the church? What have we seen so far, and what do Scripture's prophecies forecast for planet Earth and those living on it?

Chapter 2

GLOBALISM AT THE GATES

The coronavirus pandemic of 2020 was not the first such plague to threaten our fragile planet. Throughout history, other contagions have triggered widespread death and destruction as far back as biblical times, including the judgments that devastated Pharaoh's Egypt and the annihilation of 185,000 in a single night.[1] In fact, plagues and pestilences can be found throughout the Bible, with some 127 references to them.[2]

The bubonic plague of 1346–1353 killed 25 million, while the Spanish Flu of the last century brought death to as many as 50 million worldwide. More recently, the scourge of HIV/AIDS has taken 35 million lives since its introduction into the mainstream in 1981.[3]

But according to Revelation, these pestilences won't be the last. Or the deadliest.

By June 2020, more than eight million cases of COVID were reported in some 200 countries worldwide. Most of those individuals have recovered, but not without 400,000 reportedly succumbing to the virus, the vast majority being the elderly with comorbidity issues.[4] But as it turns out, the loss of life, though the most devastating statistic, was not the only fallout from this pandemic. According to the World Trade Organization, global trade also plummeted to its lowest levels in four years, bringing the world's economy to a virtual standstill.[5] It was then predicted that international commerce would eventually be reduced by as much as one-third.[6]

A Global Reset

This then set off yet another aftershock. Having appeared like an unforeseen meteor out of the blue, within weeks of the coronavirus pandemic, world leaders began viewing this predicament as a golden opportunity to sound calls for global unity. In the heat of the outbreak, former secretary-general of the United Nations Ban Ki-moon of South Korea cited the virus's impact on "every corner of the world." His solution? "To combat this historic threat, [world] leaders must urgently put aside narrow nationalism and short-term, selfish considerations to work together in the common interest of all humanity."[7]

Ki-moon also urged all leaders to immediately begin developing a "global governance system" (led by the UN, of course) that would directly address this international crisis. He called upon the united efforts of the G20 leadership, the International Monetary Fund, and the World Bank to join in with their support. An appeal to "human rights, solidarity, and justice" was made in an effort to stimulate our shared "responsibility as global citizens."[8]

Currently, Ki-moon is the deputy chair of "The Elders," an independent group of international leaders "working together for peace, justice, and human rights."[9] Key elements of their global agenda include multilateral cooperation among nations, peace, universal health coverage, and battling climate change, toward "justice for all."[10]

Echoing Ban in this push for a centralized power was the former prime minister of Great Britain, Gordon Brown, who boldly called for a "temporary form of global government to deal with the coronavirus crisis."[11] Other likeminded organizations also see a centralized governing authority as essential to combating injustice, the healthcare crisis, and, predictably, climate change. The real enemy, they say, is *nationalism*.[12] Therefore, a one-world alliance is the only answer.

Joining in with this sentiment, the mostly European group Democracy Without Borders has, among its intentions, to register all individuals as "citizens of the world." The group has also stated what they see as a critical need for a one-world government:

> We are related to one another and dependent upon one another, and everything is related to everything…If we do not take this historical opportunity, future generations will not forgive us. Unrestrained nationalism has already done enough damage. It's time for change and the time is *now*.[13]

Casting off capitalism for a socialist new world order is what the World Economic Forum is proposing. At a virtual June 2020 meeting, some of the world's most powerful business leaders convened, concluding that what our planet needs most is a "global reset." This ambitious vision will "adopt more socialistic policies, such as wealth taxes, additional regulations and massive Green New Deal-like government programs."

Promising to revamp "all aspects of societies and economies," this universal agenda calls on all nations to unite and participate.[14] And they're not passive about it. Prince Charles of Great Britain asserted, "We have a golden opportunity to seize something good from this crisis—its unprecedented shockwaves may well make people more receptive to big visions of change." Later he added, "It is an opportunity we have never had before and may never have again."[15]

Okay, wait a minute. What's so wrong with the world coming

together to fight a common enemy? I mean, isn't that a good thing? Isn't that precisely what many nations did during both World Wars? Is it so bad for the world to unite around a shared cause that benefits all nations? Why is globalization so demonized in Christian circles? Who among us doesn't want world peace, justice, and security for all mankind? Seems like an honorable and noble pursuit, right? To work together toward a day when everyone lives in equality, peace, and unity with everyone else? Sounds desirable, even noble, doesn't it? Like John Lennon's song "Imagine" come to life.

Unity = survival. Unity = peace. Unity = prosperity. How could we object to that?

Rome Reincarnated

To begin answering these questions, let's acknowledge that unity can be a very honorable and mutually beneficial pursuit. True, had the Allied powers during World War II not come together and defeated their common enemy, an entire generation would have suffered under the iron fist of a fascist Führer. So, admittedly, in principle alone, a greater good can be achieved if all nations cooperate in battling something as deadly as a universal pandemic. Such cooperation even sounds wise.

And then reality sets in. While a global government might sound like a good idea, we must consider the fact that it would almost certainly not operate upon a Judeo-Christian view of morality and justice. Rather, due to divergent cultural values and conflicting worldviews, it would, both by necessity and design, utilize a moral code that is subject to the ever-changing definitions of truth prevalent in our day. Instead of appealing to the Creator's prescribed blueprint for humanity and government, any new world order formed today will be informed by the darkened minds of those who hold positions of power. It is these very nations, Scripture says, that are destined to devise a vain thing, taking their counsel together "against the LORD and against His Anointed" (Psalm 2:1-2).

Further, this type of government, created in the context of a global crisis, would, by definition, rob individual countries of their sovereignty. Such proposed one-world governments would undoubtedly be founded on the dual principles of socialism and world citizenship—in other words, a world where individual rights are stripped away for the sake of the common good of the collective. History reminds us that such conglomerates are breeding grounds for dictatorships and totalitarian rule. In the name of peace and safety, this brand of global government requires its citizens to surrender their rights to the state.

In such an environment, nationalism is dismissed as narrow-minded and a relic of a bygone era. Practically, what is prescribed for nations is then also true for individuals. No one person, or nation, is, on paper, greater than another. And with public health and climate change as their lead causes, globalists hope to sell the world on their vision.[16] Supposedly, all citizens will be equal under this unifying regime and profit equally. But again, history teaches us that such regimes (for example, the Soviet Union, China, Cuba) end up creating an elite class that grows rich and rules over the masses of commoners. That, however, has not discouraged those who advocate globalism. Bible prophecy tells us that a one-world administration will become reality in the end times. This government will unite the nations like at no other time in history. Realistically speaking, how could this happen? Simple. All that is needed is a global crisis severe enough to mandate such a merging of the nations. More about that in chapter 8.

So how does Scripture describe this coming global kingdom? What will this future one-world government look like? Both Daniel and Revelation give us concrete clues concerning the nature and formation of this last-days empire:

There will be a fourth kingdom as strong as iron; inasmuch as iron crushes and shatters all things, so, like iron that breaks in pieces, it will crush and break all these in pieces. In that you saw the feet and toes, partly of potter's clay and partly of iron, it will be a divided kingdom; but it will have in it the toughness of iron, inasmuch as you saw the iron mixed with common clay. As the toes of the feet were partly of iron and partly of pottery, so some of the kingdom will be strong and part of it will be brittle. And in that you saw the iron mixed with common clay, they will combine with one another in the seed of men; but they will not adhere to one another, even as iron does not combine with pottery (Daniel 2:40-43).

After this I kept looking in the night visions, and behold, a fourth beast, dreadful and terrifying and extremely strong; and it had large iron teeth. It devoured and crushed and trampled down the remainder with its feet; and it was different from all the beasts that were before it, and it had ten horns. While I was contemplating the horns, behold, another horn, a little one, came up among them, and three of the first horns were pulled out by the roots before it; and behold, this horn possessed eyes like the eyes of a man and a mouth uttering great boasts (Daniel 7:7-8).

As for the ten horns, out of this kingdom ten kings will arise; and another will arise after them, and he will be different from the previous ones and will subdue three kings (Daniel 7:24).

Amazingly, 2,600 years ago, Daniel was given the interpretation of King Nebuchadnezzar's dream-vision. In it, he saw a statute representing four successive world kingdoms. We now know from history the identities of these kingdoms: Babylon (head of gold),

Medo-Persia (chest of silver), Greece (belly and thighs of bronze), and Rome (legs of iron). Especially noteworthy is that Daniel described the feet and toes of this final kingdom as being made "partly of iron and partly of clay" (Daniel 2:33). Most prophecy experts interpret this to mean the final form of the Roman Empire will be both weak and strong (2:42). This could also be referring to strong nations aligning themselves with weaker ones.

Later, in chapter 7, Daniel was given a vision, which he related to Babylon's King Belshazzar. In this explanation, he interpreted the ten toes of Daniel 2:42 as ten *horns*, or ten *kings* (7:7, 24).

Why is this so interesting? Because the Roman Empire never existed as a ten-king entity. Instead, the empire came to an end before any such division could be formed. Eventually, history records the Roman Empire did indeed split into two (the legs in Daniel 2:33) and gradually declined, with the western part falling in AD 476 and the eastern succumbing in 1453. By contrast, Daniel's vision states this ten-king configuration of the Roman Empire will be destroyed instantaneously by Messiah's kingdom (2:34-35, 44-45).

If the Roman Empire has yet to exist as a ten-nation alliance, Daniel's prophecy must still await a future fulfillment. I believe it will come to fruition during the coming seven-year tribulation. Revelation 13 and 17 confirm that ten kings (symbolically represented by ten horns) will form a final world government (Revelation 13:1; 17:3, 12-13). Because of Daniel's prophecy, we can reasonably conclude that this government will occupy the same regional geography that the Roman Empire did.

The Antichrist, whom I will address more extensively in chapter 4, will emerge onto history's geopolitical scene to head up this end-times international coalition. According to the Bible, he will face some opposition from three of those kings and will swiftly dispense of them, possibly killing them (Daniel 7:8, 24). After replacing them, the remaining rulers will unconditionally submit to the Antichrist's authority, even turning their kingdoms over to this man (Revelation 17:12-13, 17). At that time, the Antichrist will officially reign over a revived Roman Empire that spans the globe (Revelation 13:3-4, 8, 12, 16).[17]

Predictably, the initial platform of this final world government will be built upon "peace and safety" (1 Thessalonians 5:3; see also Daniel 9:27; Revelation 6:2), but will soon turn to tyranny and dictatorial domination (Revelation 13:14-17).

Many have speculated about which countries will be part of this ten-nation confederation. Today we are seeing several simultaneous attempts at unifying the nations over shared causes and for the common good of all mankind. There's the G7, the G20, and of course the European Union, which is presently made up of 27 countries. It is unclear what the precise positions and conditions of nations will be at the time of Antichrist's rise to prominence.

However, what we do know is that Antichrist's empire will be represented by ten kings or nations (Revelation 13:1; 17:3, 12-13). It is conceivable that amidst the global chaos of that tumultuous period, multiple nations will come together, consolidating to form a single national entity. In addition, some stronger, more powerful nations may annex others, "representing" them in this new world collaboration. Whatever the case, the most dominating expression of this empire will be seen during the second half of the seven-year tribulation.

Babylon Rebirthed

The Bible states that the headquarters for this new world order will be in "Babylon" (Revelation 17). Formerly a dominant force in the ancient world, Babylon will once again be a great religious and commercial city-system (Revelation 17–18). The apostle John pictured her as a prostitute riding on the back of the beast (Antichrist). He wrote,

> [The angel] carried me away in the Spirit into a wilderness; and I saw a woman sitting on a scarlet beast, full of blasphemous names, having seven heads and ten horns. And the woman was clothed in purple and scarlet, and adorned with gold and precious stones and pearls, having in her hand a gold cup of abominations and of the unclean things of her immorality, and on her forehead a name was written, a mystery, "Babylon the great, the mother of harlots and of the abominations of the earth" (Revelation 17:3-5).

This immoral woman, the religion of Babylon, will seduce and intoxicate the people of Earth with her apostate religion. The fact that she rides on top of the beast signifies that she will not only be supported by the Antichrist but will also initially overshadow him in some way.

In Greek mythology, Zeus is said to have transformed himself into a white bull in order to attract the attention of a young Phoenician princess named Europa. After coaxing her onto his back he rode away to an island, where he raped her. Curiously, this very depiction of a woman riding a bull (or beast) has gained prominence in the present-day European Union. It appears on the Greek two-euro coin, German currency and phone cards, a British stamp, and even a *Time* magazine cover depicting a united Europe.[18] Were you to travel to Brussels, Belgium today and go to the Council of the European Union building, you would see a large sculpture of this same Europa riding a bull. Is this mere coincidence or prophetic convergence?

There has also been considerable discussion about whether the apostle John was writing about a literal rebuilt Babylon in the last days, or the name Babylon was speaking in symbolic terms of a different city. Peter does use the name symbolically to describe Rome in 1 Peter 5:13, and some see the same in a description that appears in Revelation 17:9: "the seven heads are seven mountains on which the woman sits." Because Rome is a city built on seven hills, this verse must be referring to Rome, right?

And yet the immediate context itself explains away that interpretation.[19] The seven *heads* (mountains) are immediately stated to be seven *kings* (nations). Five of them had already "fallen" (17:10) at the time of John's writing. Historically, this would correlate to Egypt, Babylon, Syria, Medo-Persia, and Greece. The angel then said that one of the kings (nations) currently "is." This would be the Roman Empire of John's day. The other king (kingdom) "has *not yet* come; and when he comes, he must remain a little while." This points to a revived Roman Empire arising in the last days.

So, if Babylon isn't Rome, what is it? Six times in Revelation, the Antichrist's capital city is called "Babylon" (14:8; 16:19; 17:5; 18:2, 10, 21). Further, Babylon is mentioned as an actual city in almost 300 different places in Scripture, second only to Jerusalem. And whenever the Old Testament mentions the name, it always refers to the literal city of Babylon. In addition, of the 404 verses in Revelation, 44 of them mention Babylon (11 percent). Though it is certainly possible that this Babylon could represent some other location, a normal, plain interpretation of those verses indicates that Antichrist's headquarters will be located in the formerly ancient and rebuilt city of Babylon.

But how is this possible? Consider this: If God can make Israel a nation again after 2,000 years of Jewish dispersion across the world (Zechariah 10:6-10), then surely Satan can rebuild one city for his Antichrist.

But why this specific city? Two main reasons. First, Babylon was originally founded under a powerful leader called Nimrod. Along with the Tower of Babel, Babylon itself represented the first global rebellion against God (Genesis 10:8-12; 11:1-9). It later became a pagan center of "religion, commerce, and government" under King Nebuchadnezzar.[20] It was also the birthplace of the pagan religious mother-child cult that eventually spread to other cultures like Assyria (Ishtar-Tammuz), Phoenicia (Astarte-Baal), Egypt (Isis-Osirus), Greece (Aphrodite-Eros), and Rome (Venus-Cupid). Both Ezekiel and Jeremiah sternly warned against paying homage to Tammuz and the "queen of heaven"—that is, Ishtar (Jeremiah 7:18-20; 44:17-19, 25; Ezekiel 8:14-15). Ultimately, Babylon represents an ancient defiance against the God of heaven.

Second, up until a partial rebuilding of the city of Babylon by Saddam Hussein, this city has remained in ruins since the days of Roman rule. Isaiah prophesied that Babylon will one day be totally decimated, "as when God overthrew Sodom and Gomorrah. It will never be inhabited or lived in from generation to generation; nor will the Arab pitch his tent there, nor will shepherds make their flocks lie down there" (Isaiah 13:19-20). However, today, more than 200,000 people live in the city, which tells us Isaiah's prophecy has not yet been fulfilled. But in the future, it will be (Revelation 14:8; 18:2). Prior to Jesus' second coming, Antichrist's Babylonian headquarters (also referred to as the "dwelling place of demons" in Revelation 18:2) will fall in *one hour* (Revelation 18:1-10, 17). When Jesus spoke about the sign of His coming, He quoted Isaiah 13:10 concerning Babylon's ultimate destruction: "Immediately after the tribulation of those days THE SUN WILL BE DARKENED, AND THE MOON WILL NOT GIVE ITS LIGHT, AND THE STARS WILL FALL from the sky, and the powers of the heavens will be shaken and then the sign of the Son of Man will appear in the sky" (Matthew 24:29-30).

I agree with the many Bible scholars who believe the ancient city of Babylon will be rebuilt by Antichrist and serve as his world head-quarters during the tribulation. Not only would this be in harmony with Satan's territorial marking of this geographical spot as a hotbed for false religion and anti-God sentiment, but there are also practical reasons that Antichrist would choose this location. There are rich oil reserves in this area, and it is strategically located between continents. It is also bordered by the banks of the Euphrates River, which, in Revelation, is associated with demonic activity and the preparation for Armageddon (Revelation 9:14-15; 16:12). So why Babylon? Two reasons: rebellion and resources.

The Devil's Day and Divine Delusion

You may be wondering, "Okay, all this is fascinating and informative. But what does any of it have to do with me right now?" Good question.

First, keep in mind that Satan does not now know, nor has he ever known, the precise timing of God's prophetic plan for the last days. Even so, many times throughout history, he has attempted to jumpstart the era of Antichrist. Why? Because the tribulation period is going to be his heyday, his time to shine. That's when he will finally be able to rule the world without restraints and be worshipped by its inhabitants. This is been his goal from the very beginning (Isaiah 14:12-14; Ezekiel 28:11-19). Even though he is the "god of this world" (2 Corinthians 4:4), Satan has never been able to implement his desired agenda. Therefore, whenever there is a global crisis, it presents him with the opportunity to once again pursue his goal of a unified and centralized global government that he can control.

Currently, the entity that comes the closest to a globally unified government is the European Union. Founded in 1957, this governing body of nations has signed numerous international treaties and even established a new European currency, the Euro. On

October 29, 2004, 25 member nations signed a new EU constitution amid great pomp at a ceremony on Capitoline Hill in Rome.[21] And in late 2009, their Lisbon Treaty permanently established the office of president of Europe, a role that is filled in two-and-a-half-year terms.[22] Global peace. A common currency. And one governing leader whose authority most closely resembles Antichrist's future rule.

I am not suggesting that the European Union is the fulfillment of Antichrist's future kingdom. But it may very well be a foreshadowing or some developmental form of it. Certainly, the spirit and symbolism of the EU is in harmony with the revived Roman Empire that is portrayed in Scripture and will one day be established under Antichrist's leadership.

For Christians, the reality that all of this will happen one day is a matter of discernment. Therefore, in these last days, it is critical for Christ's followers to recognize that (1) a one-world government is coming, and (2) the devil is continually seeking to hasten its arrival in every way he can. He not only lies in wait for this government but also places the bait for it.

A second reason why all this matters to us now is that Paul prophesied that God will place the world under a great delusion during the last days (2 Thessalonians 2:9-11). This delusion will be so severe that the people of Earth will easily embrace satanic deception and Antichrist's lies. But why? Two reasons: (1) Satan will convince them using "all power and signs and false wonders" (2 Thessalonians 2:9). And (2) God will then send His own "*deluding influence* so that they will believe what is false" (2:11).

This may sound a bit odd, but God's justification for doing this is because people will refuse to "receive the love of the truth so as to be saved" prior to this time (2:10). It's similar to the way He hardened Pharaoh's heart (Exodus 4:21; Romans 9:17). As a believer in

Christ, God wants you to recognize how the spirit of Antichrist is at work *today* in your world and culture (1 John 4:1-3; see also 2:18, 22). Satan is deceiving people about God's truth and blinding them to Jesus' gospel (2 Corinthians 4:4).

> The Bible tells us that true and righteous unity won't be achieved until Christ's millennial kingdom.

Presently, the vast majority of humanity is reaping the awful consequences of continually rejecting God's truth. These consequences lead them into further darkness, which, in turn, causes them to speculate in ignorance about what is real and true (Romans 1:18-22). Ultimately, after pursuing their own pleasures in sinful lifestyles, God delivers them over to a depraved, nonfunctioning mind, which leads to all sorts of evil and sin (Romans 1:24-32). We cannot afford to be naïve concerning the world around us and the deluded condition of the unsaved.

Third, as confirmed by Bible prophecy, we know the world will never fully unite until Antichrist appears. Every effort toward globalization is masterminded by Satan, the architect of the Tower of Babel. This final one-world government will serve as yet another refrain of his original rebellion against God.

The Bible tells us that true and righteous unity won't be achieved until Christ's millennial kingdom (Zechariah 2:10-11; Revelation 20). In the meantime, watch for more talk about a new world order, planet management, and world unity. People are incrementally coming together and becoming bonded more and more by a common enmity against God. And their vision of a godless globalism anxiously awaits at the gates, longing for the time when it will enter history's narrative and become reality—just as is foretold in the book of Revelation.

With the spirit of globalism growing, and nationalism (and patriotism) being portrayed as a vestige of yesteryear, the question may arise whether it's okay for a believer in Jesus to engage in such loyalist activities as pledging allegiance to the flag or singing "The Star-Spangled Banner." I believe the answer is yes. A pledge to our flag is not blind obedience to the State (as in Nazi Germany), but simply a promise to be a responsible citizen in our country, one which was founded as "one nation, under God." It's okay to love your country and to extol the Judeo-Christian virtues upon which it was founded. What you must also keep in mind, though, is that we in America are not God's "chosen people," and the United States is not what God had in mind when He spoke to Solomon, "If…My people who are called by My name humble themselves and pray and seek My face and turn from their wicked ways, then I will hear from heaven , will forgive their sin and will heal their land" (2 Chronicles 7:13-14). We are not Israel, or in any sense the "new" Israel. We are a Gentile nation, but unlike most such nations, ours was uniquely founded on biblical principles and virtues.

Second, America is one country that has traditionally stood in the way of globalism. By asserting her sovereignty, we are a part of the resistance to the expanding spirit of a one-world system.

And third, patriotism and love of country are nowhere prohibited in Scripture. Rather, God wants us to acknowledge and live in light of the fact that our true "citizenship is in heaven, from which also we eagerly wait for a Savior, the Lord Jesus Christ" (Philippians 3:20). This Earth, and country, are not our real home. This truth is made especially clear in the chaotic climate of these last days.

Chapter 3

CAESAR AND GOD

In George Orwell's classic *Nineteen Eighty-Four*, the author introduces us to a character called Big Brother, the dictatorial leader of Oceania. Seemingly omnipresent posters bear his image everywhere, proclaiming, "Big Brother Is Watching You." Oceania's thought police closely monitor the conversations and actions of its citizens. It's a world where government is god. Written in the wake of World War II with Hitler's Nazi regime and Stalinism as the background, *Nineteen Eighty-Four* is a secular prophetic warning against the evils of totalitarianism. This dystopian novel has become synonymous with political control and governmental overreach.

Borrowing concepts from the fascist cultures of his day, Orwell coined terms such as *Newspeak*, the government's language propaganda machine. Newspeak essentially curtails free thought and expression while replacing them with the party's own words, doctrines, and dictates. Another Orwellian concept is *doublethink*, or holding to two contradictory beliefs while sincerely believing they are both true.

Big Brother's propaganda strategy is designed to brainwash the public's thinking, gradually convincing the masses that "War Is Peace," "Freedom Is Slavery," and "Ignorance Is Strength." And the bigger the lie, the greater the success in persuading people of that lie. Doublespeak is also employed to deliberately obscure, distort, disguise, or redefine words in order to make them more easily acceptable to the general public. Basically, doublespeak makes lies sound truer and murder seem more "respectable."[1]

Redefining Reality for the Masses

Some of what Orwell wrote about back in 1949 has found its way into our own culture. Though we obviously have yet to transform into the totalitarian state Orwell envisioned, biblically discerning Christians can recognize the prophetic implications and overtones portrayed in this bestselling book. With the passing of time, many of Orwell's fictional portrayals have woven their way into the fabric of our cultural consciousness. That's because Satan is the master of doublespeak, a deception especially convincing to darkened minds and undiscerning believers. And he has spun his deceptive web of lies into mainstream thought so subtly and effectively that our present generation is thoroughly convinced of this reimagined reality.

What are some of the ways we see this happening today?

- Murder of the unborn isn't really *murder*. It's popularly known as "healthcare," "reproductive freedom," and a "woman's right over her own body."

- A fetus isn't actually a *child*, but rather a "clump of cells," an unwanted cyst or growth. Today, killing an unborn human up until the moment of birth is not only legally allowed, it is funded, protected, promoted, and gloriously celebrated worldwide. In 2015, the hashtag #shoutyourabortion went viral, inspiring parades, parties, T-shirts, and books created for those who proudly reveled in having their babies destroyed inside their wombs.[2]

- Homosexuality is no longer viewed as unnatural, as being opposed to God's design for sex and marriage (Genesis 18–19; Romans 1:18-32; 1 Corinthians 6:9-11).

- Marriage between members of the same sex has been declared to be a basic human "right," according to the US Supreme Court.[3] No longer is this considered a betrayal of biology, a perversion of morality, and a sabotage to civilization. It's *law*.

- Gender is now considered fluid and malleable and has been detached from its original biological definition, which said gender is determined and fixed at conception. Rather, it is viewed as a construct of thought, feelings, and life experiences.

- Men now identify as women (and vice versa) by merely speaking their preferred gender into existence. Freedom is granted to individuals (by the government and culture) to reinvent and redefine their sexual identity. A refusal to recognize and affirm this new reality can result in fines or jail time for the noncompliant.[4]

- Reality itself is no longer based in or known by facts (as we have "mistakenly" presumed since the dawn of time). Instead, reality is what *you* perceive it to be.

- Moral standards are relative ("What's right for you may not be right for me"). Consequently, there are no longer any moral absolutes (that self-contradictory statement, of course, being the sole exception to this rule).

Contemporary culture and government now sanction, support,

and celebrate all the above, protecting many of them under the law. And yet all these redefinitions and distortions are ultimately lies that are made possible through psychological manipulation and a denial of reality.

And what happens to those who dare to speak the truth? They are condemned as dissenters and are demonized by the immoral majority who view themselves as enlightened. Ultimately, their aggregate delusion turns them into "thought dictators" who project their altered realities on the blank-slate minds of the unthinking masses.

All of this is a chilling foreshadow of the global deception that will occur in the last days prior to the rapture (Matthew 24:4, 8-12, 24; 2 Thessalonians 2:1-12; 2 Timothy 3:1-5). Good is bad. Bad is good. And you are god.

We can expect delusional doublespeak to worsen in the days ahead because government powers are resorting to it more and more. As a general rule, the greater the crises in our world, the bigger government's role becomes in our lives. Sometimes this can work positively, as in the case of federal disaster relief following a hurricane. But it can also work to our disadvantage, intruding and seeking to enact policy and changes that hurt our freedoms and curtail basic rights.

In the wake of the initial COVID-19 crisis, governments around the world scrambled to enact sweeping guidelines that significantly affected the daily lives of their citizens. The residual effect of these mandates eventually prompted many to question the state of freedom worldwide. With some 200-plus countries affected by the crisis, virtually no one was immune from the restrictions imposed.[5]

Fragile Freedom

In America, we have traditionally enjoyed the freedoms our

founding fathers mapped out for us in the Constitution, the Declaration of Independence, and the Bill of Rights. These include privileges such as freedom of expression (free speech and freedom of the press), freedom of association (freedom of religion, movement, and assembly), freedom from seizure of property, a free economic structure, and a fair legal system that provides us equality under the law and before the law.

While these freedoms form the skeletal system of America's infrastructure, there are no guarantees exempting our country from drifting away from her original guiding documents and self-evident truths. That's because governments are run by people, including incompetent or ill-intentioned officials who make colossal, course-altering errors. In recent years, we have witnessed leaders at virtually every level of government pushing and promoting ideological and political agendas that chip away at our freedoms and exert more control over our personal lives.

During the corona pandemic, we saw some of these freedoms threatened. And we are still experiencing the aftershocks from these restrictions. Governments shut down churches, schools, businesses, beaches, and parks. Graduations, funerals, and family gatherings were canceled. New fathers were not permitted in hospital delivery rooms. Neighborhood get-togethers were physically disbanded by police. All this, and yet at the same time, large protests and mass demonstrations were openly permitted without question. The contradictions were glaringly obvious and hinted at a hidden agenda.

Doublespeak.

Specified businesses were suddenly deemed "nonessential" and forced to close. As a result, livelihoods were put on hold, with many small businesses never to open again. Lifelong investments were lost. What further confused the public was the blurred line between businesses deemed essential and those that were not. For example, in Kentucky, drive-through liquor purchases were permitted, while drive-through church services were not.[6]

In California, Governor Gavin Newsom threatened to declare martial law if citizens failed to comply with business restrictions.[7] And his ongoing battle with California churches drew national attention. Such threats, restrictions, and fines aroused further suspicion that a deeper political or spiritual scheme was at play.

During this time, all 50 states declared health emergencies—all in the name of public safety. But many people questioned whether their governments were telling the whole truth concerning the dangers of COVID-19. Allegations of inflated case numbers and doctored death certificates surfaced.[8] This gave birth to a host of conspiracy theories about what was really going on behind the scenes. At first Americans were patient and compliant, but with continued restrictions limiting their movement and freedom, they soon grew restless. And though the majority adhered to social mandates by staying at home and wearing masks when in public, as time went on, more and more became part of an outcry for government officials to take steps back to normalcy.

In all of this, many people wondered: If one invisible virus can effectively shut down the entire world through governmental initiatives, what else could bureaucracies justify, given the right crisis?

Even so, America did not reach the level of government control experienced by other countries. For example, the entire nation of Italy was declared a "red zone." Christian friends there informed me that an official, government-approved certificate was required just for people to leave their homes for anything other than an emergency or officially approved business.

In China, whole cities were barricaded and quarantined, essentially placing citizens under house arrest. State police forcibly dragged those suspected of infection out of their cars and homes, handcuffed and put them in hazmat trucks, and transported them to what amounted to prison hospitals. And anyone who dared speak against the directives was also arrested.[9]

Fortunately, in America, we have state principalities that can check certain federal powers, if need be. Even so, we have already seen such overreach into businesses—one vivid example of this is the attempt to force private religious employers to provide contraceptive services against their beliefs.[10] Further, unchecked federal power could also seek to revoke tax-exempt status for religious nonprofits and churches who failed to conform to morally based federal mandates.[11] At any given moment, a sitting administration hostile to Christianity may suddenly determine that faith-based institutions must comply with intrusive, immoral federal mandates.

And even though our Constitutional amendment process can help prevent this overreach, there are still ways around government checks and balances. In 2020, citing Title VII of the Civil Rights Act of 1964, the US Supreme Court ruled that employers could not fire an employee because he or she is homosexual or transgender. In other words, the nation's highest court says men who believe they are women now have the same "civil rights" as those born of a particular race. Therefore, legally, to consider yourself a transgender is on par with being born black (that is, a person's self-made gender choice is to be treated the same as a person's God-ordained race). What surprised many is that Justice Neil M. Gorsuch (a Trump appointee), whom many had lauded as holding to a conservative approach to a justice's role in the court, sided with his liberal colleagues on this issue.

Just five years earlier, under the Obama administration, the US Supreme Court recognized gay marriage as a "basic human right." Upon hearing the decision, then-President Obama celebrated in the Oval Office. That evening, as darkness fell on Washington (literally and spiritually), he lit up the White House in the rainbow colors of the gay flag.

But while the 2020 ruling about Title VII was viewed as a major victory for the homosexual-transgender community, it prompted some, like Southern Baptist public policy spokesman Russell Moore, to write that the decision would have "seismic implications" for religious freedom.[12]

But how? Are these government decisions really such big deals? Are Christians overinflating the aftershocks of such rulings? Do they really threaten us? What difference does it make if our government legislates morality? Don't all laws already do that?

Here's why it really is a big deal. Part of the significance of decisions like the Title VII ruling is that they further confirm that Christians are losing the culture wars over morality and sexuality.[13] Also, in making such rulings, our government deliberately ignores and defies biblical mandates and truths concerning the traditional family unit and civilization itself, elevating a person's unbiblical—and thus immoral—preference to civil rights status. In this way, potentially anything that is naturally and morally abnormal or offensive could be justified by simply relabeling it as a civil right. And this likely will continue to happen. Next up: Watch for heinous sins such as pedophilia[14] and multiple marriage partners (including "throuples")[15] to move incrementally toward normalization as well. In fact, efforts are already underway to destigmatize these lifestyles.[16]

Led by grassroots campaigns, activists will first gain sympathy, then favor, in psychological and medical circles (giving them a level of credibility). Pedophilia is already being argued as just another sexual orientation.[17] And should we continue down this path, eventually a grown man will be able to legally marry a young boy, and a woman can be in a marriage relationship with two or more men.

All based on the rationale that *love is love*.

The redefinition of societal and moral standards teaches us an important lesson about culture, government, and individuals. When Christian virtues such as equality, love, and tolerance are hijacked and then redefined, reimagined, and repackaged according to a carnal culture, this is the expected outcome. And Christians are mandated to abide by these rulings—thus losing their religious freedoms. This has also forced churches and whole denominations to determine how they will respond, and many have already split over the issue of same-sex marriage.[18]

Big Brother Is Watching

Morality. Laws. Culture. Government.

Could all this be part of preparing humanity for the end times, when the whole world will be under one government's control? Possibly. But not everyone is drinking the Kool-Aid. In 2020, a conservative Catholic contingency out of Rome released a manifesto claiming that the coronavirus was merely a pretext designed to "deprive citizens around the world of their fundamental freedoms and to promote a world government."[19]

The manifesto continues:

> We have reason to believe, on the basis of official data on the incidence of the epidemic as related to the number of deaths, that there are powers interested in creating panic among the world's population with the sole aim of permanently imposing unacceptable forms of restriction on freedoms, of controlling people and of tracking their movements. The imposition of these illiberal measures is a disturbing prelude to the realization of a *world government beyond all control.*[20]

This bold manifesto also expressed suspicions and fears regarding digital tracking systems and any other methods of surveillance upon citizens, as well as powerful entities or individuals using the corona-virus to gain political influence or control. It concludes,

> Let us not allow centuries of Christian civilization to be erased under the pretext of a virus, and an *odious technological tyranny* to be established, in which nameless and faceless people can decide the fate of the world by confining us to a virtual reality. If this is the plan to which the powers of this earth intend to make us yield, know that Jesus Christ, King and Lord of History, has promised that "the gates of Hell shall not prevail" (Mt 16:18).[21]

Meanwhile, back in America, Franklin Graham echoed the same sentiment, stating, "It's becoming more obvious to people that the response of some in the government is not just about protecting lives, but it's about control."[22]

How, then, are we as Christians to respond to what appears to be a growing intrusion of government into our lives? What coming crisis or excuse will authorities use to curtail more of our freedoms and potentially muzzle expressions of our faith? If they can mandate home confinement and masks to be worn in public, how long before an identifying patch or mark is implemented? When does contact tracing (on your phone) lead to restricting your access to stores because of suspected virus or infection risks?

To effectively answer those questions, we must turn to the only reliable and infallible source that can adequately address them—God's Word. Politicians, judges, and legislators cannot help Christians here. For us to be salt and light in a dark and decaying world, we must hear straight from God.

Render and Respect

In Romans 13, Paul outlines both the purpose of government as well as our response to it:

Every person is to be in subjection to the governing authorities. For there is no authority except from God, and those
which exist are established by God. Therefore whoever
resists authority has opposed the ordinance of God; and
they who have opposed will receive condemnation upon
themselves. For rulers are not a cause of fear for good behavior, but for evil. Do you want to have no fear of authority? Do what is good and you will have praise from the
same; for it is a minister of God to you for good. But if you
do what is evil, be afraid; for it does not bear the sword for
nothing; for it is a minister of God, an avenger who brings
wrath on the one who practices evil. Therefore it is necessary to be in subjection, not only because of wrath, but
also for conscience' sake. For because of this you also pay
taxes, for rulers are servants of God, devoting themselves
to this very thing. Render to all what is due them: tax to
whom tax is due; custom to whom custom; fear to whom
fear; honor to whom honor (verses 1-7).

The first principle we observe in this passage is that we are commanded to submit to governing authorities. Concepts like submission and subjection are not popular in a culture that values and
prioritizes personal choice, self-love, and self-rule over all else. We
see "subjection" used 43 times in the New Testament, and in reference to believers, it signifies a voluntary placing of oneself under
another's authority. It's a military term that means "to follow, or line
up under a superior officer."

It's the same word used in Scripture to describe

- the subjection of all things under Christ's feet (1 Corinthians 15:27)

- the subjection of Christ to the Father (1 Corinthians 15:28)

- the church's subjection to Christ (Ephesians 5:24)

- the wife's subjection to her husband (Colossians 3:18)
- our own subjection to God (James 4:7)

Fortunately, whenever God gives us a command, He typically provides the reason for it. Here, Paul said that every existing governing authority exists because God established it. Therefore, Paul's Holy Spirit-inspired logic led him to conclude that to oppose these authorities is to oppose an ordinance that God Himself has ordained (Romans 13:2). Bear in mind that Paul wrote his words in the context of a godless, pagan Roman Empire ruled by depraved governors and decadent Caesars. Even so, generally speaking, most civilized governments are committed to establishing order and enforcing the rule of law. They exist to punish those who practice evil and to instill healthy fear in everyone else.

Biblically speaking, a government's foundational role includes bringing wrath upon those who practice evil and protecting law-abiding citizens, partially through instilling the fear of retribution in those who would consider doing such evil (verses 3-4). However, when government fails to do this, crime and lawlessness increase. And this is precisely what we saw amid the militant anarchist riots of 2020 in cities like Seattle, Minneapolis, Portland, and Kenosha. Hundreds of businesses were burned to the ground and downtown sectors were commandeered in futile attempts to establish utopian communes. Little to nothing was done to stem the chaos, revealing a dereliction of duty among the mayors and governors of those localities.

For followers of Jesus, the two motivations for submitting to government are to avoid wrath and to obey God (verse 5). This is why we pay taxes, respect law enforcement personnel, pray for leaders, and honor those to whom honor is due (verse 7).[23]

Paul, in his letter to Titus, instructed him to teach the church to be subject to rulers, to authorities, and to be obedient (Titus 3:1). Peter exhorts us,

> Submit yourselves for the Lord's sake to every human institution, whether to a king as the one in authority, or to governors as sent by him for the punishment of evildoers and the praise of those who do right. For such is the will of God, that by doing right you silence the ignorance of foolish people. Act as free people, and do not use your freedom as a covering for evil, but use it as bond-servants of God. Honor all people, love the brotherhood, fear God, honor the king (1 Peter 2:13-17).[24]

"King" here refers to national government. Peter assigns the same principles about submission to servants in their relationships to their masters (2:18-20), which is the closest parallel to the modern-day workplace. And fortunately, our supreme model and example in all this is Jesus, who suffered under and submitted to His governmental accusers, all the while entrusting Himself to His Father, "who judges righteously" (2:21-23).

From those verses, it's clear that Christians are to live compliant, peaceable lives under their governments. But is it ever permissible for a Christian to dissent and disobey? Can believers righteously defy that which their government dictates to them?

Reject and Refuse

Relevant questions. The short answer is yes, and here's why: Whenever human government commands us to violate Scripture, our own conscience, or our loyalty to the Lord Jesus, defiance becomes our only option.

God's Word provides numerous examples of individuals who appealed to, resisted, and even blatantly and publicly disobeyed the governing authorities. Admittedly, doing this may not be that simple, easy, or clear-cut. God's people must use great care and discernment when it comes to civil disobedience.

For example, the apostle Paul respectfully argued for his innocence before governors Felix and Festus, later appealing to King Agrippa, and ultimately to Caesar himself (Acts 24–26). Nero was Caesar from AD 54 to 68, during the time when Paul wrote to the believers in Rome. When Rome burned in AD 64, Nero blamed the Christians, subsequently igniting a firestorm of persecution and martyrdom for our first-century brothers and sisters.

However, some individuals in Scripture recognized when making an appeal would do them no good. Their circumstances forced them into one of two choices: submit or defy. Surrender or disobey. Live or risk imprisonment or death. So when is it okay to say, "Enough is enough"? Or to proclaim, "No, I will not bow"?

Consider that:

- Hebrew midwives refused to kill Jewish babies when commanded by Pharaoh to do so (Exodus 1:1-20).

- When the Jewish captives in Babylon were ordered to worship Nebuchadnezzar's golden image, three Hebrew lads—Hananiah, Mishael, and Azariah (better known as Shadrach, Meshach, and Abednego)—refused to fall down before the golden image, even upon threat of death. You are probably familiar with their story. In the end, on account of their faith, they wouldn't budge or bow. And by God's protective power, they did not burn (Daniel 3).

- Daniel continued praying to God even when directly forbidden to do so. He was turned in to the king, who had him thrown into the lions' den (Daniel 6).

- When Peter and John were brought before the Jewish elders of their day, they were commanded "not to speak or teach at all in the name of Jesus" (Acts 4:18). Their response was epic, one for the ages: "Whether it is right in the sight of God to give heed to you rather than to God, you be the judge; for we cannot stop speaking what we have seen and heard" (verses 19-20).

- In Acts 5, Peter and the apostles were given strict orders by the Jewish religious authorities to stop teaching in Jesus' name. Their reply? With one voice they declared, "We must obey God rather than men" (Acts 5:27-29). In other words, "No. N-O. We're not going to do that. Period. End of discussion."

Were these easy decisions? No. But the right call? Absolutely.

In the days leading up to the American Revolution, delegates from the Colonies gathered at the Second Virginia Convention. The purpose of the gathering was to discuss their response to King George III's unwillingness to entertain their grievances regarding unrelenting taxation. Among the delegates present at St. John's Church that day were future American legends, including George Washington and Thomas Jefferson, along with six others who would, in about a year, sign the Declaration of Independence.

Well aware that war was a forgone conclusion, a 38-year-old and well-respected lawyer named Patrick Henry stood before his fellow Virginians and delivered what proved to be a historically pivotal speech. Citing the amassing of British troops all across the new colonies, he correctly concluded, "They are meant for *us*; they can be meant for no other!" He continued, arguing,

> Our petitions have been slighted, our remonstrances have produced additional violence and insult; our supplications have been disregarded; and we have been spurned, with contempt, from the foot of the throne…we must fight! I repeat it, sir, we must fight! An appeal to arms and to the God of Hosts is all that is left us!

The veins in Henry's neck began to bulge.

> The war is actually begun! The next gale that sweeps from the north will bring to our ears the clash of resounding arms! Our brethren are already in the field! Why stand we here idle? What is it that gentlemen wish? What would they have? Is life so dear, or peace so sweet, as to be purchased at the price of chains and slavery?

Dramatically, he held his wrists together as though chained, raising them heavenward. And in a "Braveheart" moment, he exclaimed, "Forbid it, Almighty God! I know not what course others may take; but as for me, give me liberty"—freeing his wrists as if breaking the chains—"or give me death!"[25]

That was nearly 250 years ago.

In God We Trust?

What citizens must sometimes do for civic or political reasons, Christians must sometimes do for spiritual or moral reasons. For both, defiance may be a necessary option.

Though we in America have never suffered under regimes like Nero's or Nazi Germany's, and centuries have passed since we resisted and cast off England's tyranny, we are now seeing more governing authorities systematically reflect the spirit of the coming age.

And this we know: In the not-too-distant future, Christians worldwide will be required once again to bow the knee to a new Caesar—Antichrist. In Revelation 20:4, we read,

> I saw thrones, and they sat on them, and judgment was given to them. And I saw the souls of those who had been beheaded because of their testimony of Jesus and because of the word of God, and those who had not worshiped the beast or his image, and had not received the mark on

their forehead and on their hand; and they came to life and reigned with Christ for a thousand years.

From the first century to this one, believers in various places across the world have been mistreated, hated, marginalized, persecuted, and killed. As I write this, the active persecution of believers by governments and radical Muslims is occurring in some 150 countries, with estimates of anywhere from 10,000 to 90,000 dying per year because of their faith in Jesus.[26] But as horrific as those statistics are, they're nothing compared to the future slaughter of those who will turn to faith in Christ during the great tribulation. The price they pay then will be in blood, and predominantly through barbaric beheading.

Governments are not divine, but they are divinely appointed. And perhaps no nation has better exemplified the fundamental ideals of what a government should be like than the United States of America.[27] Without question, we in America have historically been blessed with unprecedented freedoms through the recognition of our basic God-given rights. We are a privileged people.

But in recent decades, we have seen the gradual deterioration of the underpinnings upon which our country was founded. This is not surprising, as humanity naturally tilts towards depravity and self-ruin. But Satan is also pushing an end-times agenda, and he's using the government to achieve his goals. Through a growing sentiment toward a one-world government, along with a deceptively alluring submission to federal mandates, we are simultaneously sliding toward Sodom while also accelerating into the era of Antichrist.

Admittedly, there are very good people in our government at every level and in every branch and department. These are men and women who have sworn allegiance not only *on* a Bible but to the principles found *within* it. However, the evil forces present in this current darkness are also fighting with unrivaled zeal and passion to achieve their godless, immoral agenda. This is not only true of far-left liberal politicians who are determined to eradicate the Judeo-Christian values upon which our government was founded, but also applies to a growing revolutionary anarchist movement that, sadly, is not going away.

Moving forward, we should anticipate an increasingly greater decay of basic decency and morality in the realm of politics, which, being translated, means any Christian or conservative candidate or appointee will be brutally opposed and vilified in an effort to keep him or her from holding public office.

> As Christians, we must regularly remind ourselves that it is the church, *not* government, that is responsible for having a positive moral influence on culture and restraining evil.

This highlights a critically important distinction between government and the church. In recent history, ever since the Reagan administration, Christians in America have tended to overinflate the role and importance of the office of president in terms of influencing the nation's moral compass. In some instances, the church has even abdicated her role in upholding a positive moral climate in our country, relying instead on conservative governing authorities to do that work for us.

But as Christians, we must regularly remind ourselves that it is the church, *not* government, that is responsible for having a positive moral influence on culture and restraining evil. When we put our trust in leaders who are sympathetic to Christian beliefs, we often relax, back off, and hand the reins to them.

However, God never said of government, "You are the light of the world." Instead, He said that of you and me (Matthew 5:14).

He never described government as being "the pillar in support of the truth," but Scripture portrays the church in this way (1 Timothy 3:15). Regrettably, Christians can end up becoming more concerned about losing elections than losing souls. Until the church recognizes that no president or administration can or will save us, we will continue to lose the battle for the soul of America.

A Christian-friendly leader, or any other government official sympathetic to Judeo-Christian values, is a welcomed blessing, but he or she can only wage a political or legal war against the forces of satanically inspired evil—those forces that seek to destroy babies in the womb, promote immoral lifestyles through legislation, redefine marriage, and grow government and its power into a multiheaded hellish hydra. Yes, we should strongly support candidates who promote righteousness and vehemently denounce those who argue on behalf of evil, murder, and immorality. It is our civic duty to cast a vote for righteousness and righteous political platforms, regardless of how imperfect a given candidate may be personally. But our government has never led a single person to Jesus Christ or changed their eternal destiny. Only the gospel can do that as believers penetrate their culture with the good news of Jesus.

Regardless of how good or effective human government is, it still has no real bearing on God's eternal kingdom. In that sense, it really doesn't matter who is president or Caesar. Christianity began, and flourished, under one of the most godless, pagan regimes the world has ever known. And according to the prophet Isaiah, ultimately, politics and presidents are irrelevant in the grand scheme of God's prophetic program (Isaiah 40:23-25). Government *does* affect our lives, but it does not and cannot hinder the gospel, for the Word of God is not imprisoned (2 Timothy 2:9). And the kingdom agenda we preach and promote "is not of this world" (John 18:36).

What Will It Cost You?

Were COVID-19 and the rampant lawlessness that followed specific fulfillments of Bible prophecy? No, but they were foreshocks to the prophesied calamities that are to come. They are mere hiccups compared to the seismic tremors that are about to hit planet Earth (Revelation 6:7-8; 9:20-21). And both were seized upon by those in government to advance agendas.

Regardless of who is president, it is quite likely we will continue to see government expand its reach into our lives, disrupting and even curtailing our freedoms. And conscious persecution of Christians will eventually find a home right here in America as we race toward Revelation 6.

According to Daniel 2, 7, and Revelation 13 and 17, a world government is coming that *will* be both totalitarian and dictatorial. And yet, as happened under Hitler's regime, the masses will think it noble and necessary to follow it, eventually paying homage to its leader. If other prophetic previews are any indication, in the days leading up to the rapture, humanity will experience a gradual and incremental conditioning toward a herd mentality, one where individual rights are eroded and replaced with increasing governmental overreach. There will come a tragic and diabolical disintegration of the relationship between the government and the people. And we are all either elements of change, frogs in the boiling water of a global kettle, or defiant Daniels destined for a den of lions.

As Jesus' disciples, we are called to live peaceful, respectful, and honorable lives in whatever culture and under whatever government we find ourselves (Romans 12:18; 1 Peter 2:17). But there may come a time when, because of conscience and commitment to God and His Word, civil disobedience is necessary, leading us to stand when all others are bowing. This means we speak up for biblical righteousness when others are silent. It means we act with integrity when others are mired in mediocrity, complacency, and deception. And like those early saints before us, we entrust ourselves to God, seeking the shelter and protection that is found beneath His wings (Psalm 91:1-10).

Polycarp was the bishop of Smyrna in the second century, and a disciple of the apostle John. In fact, he was likely the last living person to personally know John. Around AD 160 at age 86, he faced the ultimate test of his life. Rome's local sheriff arrested two of his household workers and tortured them into revealing Polycarp's whereabouts. Upon his arrest, Polycarp petitioned his captors for an hour of solitude in prayer, which they granted. That hour of prayer stretched into two, after which he was taken to an arena. There, a Roman proconsul confirmed his identity, then addressed him: "Swear by the fortune of Caesar. Repent, and say, down with the atheists [Christians]…Reproach Christ, and I will set you free."

The aged Polycarp responded, "Eighty-six years have I served Him, and He has done me no wrong. How then can I blaspheme my King and my Savior?"

After being threatened further with wild animals and fire, Polycarp stood resolute, declaring, "Why are you waiting? Bring on whatever you want."[28]

And they burned him alive.

As governments worldwide swell their ranks, intruding deeper into their citizens' lives and infringing on their rights, we believers must be discerning, recognizing the spirit of the age and that the hope of our deliverance is near. And like those first-century believers, we must draw strength and encouragement from one another as we "see the day drawing near" (Hebrews 10:25), unmoved by the winds of an evil culture or government.

Chapter 4

TECHNOLOGY AND SATAN'S SUPERMAN

Months into the corona madness, my wife and I went shopping at a nearby retail store. In addition to businesses limiting the number of customers inside it at any given time, there was also an overall weird vibe that came from the unseen dividing line between those wearing masks and those choosing not to. Being a member of the latter group, I approached the doors of a certain major clothing store only to be greeted by a sign that read, "Masks required for all employees and customers." Shaking my head, I looked to my wife, who produced a spare mask from her purse. Upon entering the store, the manager greeted us, quickly stating that this retail chain would no longer be accepting cash.

"You're kidding, right?" I said.

"No, sir. I am not," he replied. "No more cash here."

"Unbelievable," I mumbled beneath my paper breathing apparatus.

As it turns out, this cashless policy and practice is gaining traction across America as part of a larger movement. In fact, it's a financial phenomenon that has been trending in other parts of the world for several years now. In 2018, digital transactions in India increased by 55 percent, compared with 4 percent in China and 23 percent in Indonesia.[1] Though experts say it's way too early to start ringing the death knell for cash, others speculate that by 2022, due to the societal and economic effects of COVID-19, we will be closer than ever before to a completely cashless society.[2]

Consider that today, 30 percent of America's transactions are digital, and more than one in ten millennials use their "digital wallet" for *every single* purchase.[3] If that trend grows, we could see cash trickle out of commerce at an even faster rate. But it doesn't stop there. The economic landscape is changing rapidly as we're transitioning from cash to swiping or inserting cards to contactless cards to digital wallets. Currently, Apple Pay and Google Pay allow transactions to be made without even touching a card to a terminal or entering a PIN.[4] Contactless payment is a pretty wild concept for anyone over the age of 40. But even this has already become yesterday's news as personal technology continues to move forward in quantum leaps. Many smartphone users utilize fingerprint and facial recognition technology to unlock their phones, and it is forecast that by 2024, biometric facial recognition will be available on 90 percent of all smartphones.[5]

Now Amazon has raised the technological stakes even higher in the world of commerce with biometric scanning, a process that allows you to make payments using *only your hand*.[6] While it can take about four seconds to insert a card or even use contactless payment, paying by hand-scan takes about 300 milliseconds! And the accuracy rate is within one ten-thousandth of 1 percent.[7]

In December of 2019, Amazon filed a patent for "a scanner device [that] is used to obtain raw images of a user's palm that is within a field of view of the scanner." The first hyper scan of images "depicts external characteristics, such as lines and creases in the user's palm, while the second set of images depicts internal anatomical structures, such as veins, bones, soft tissue, or other structures beneath the epidermis of the skin."[8]

It's for Your Own Good

And why are we moving so rapidly in this direction? There are five main reasons:

1. Protection Against Theft and Fraud

As long as there is a physical object necessary for making transactions, such as a card or a phone, it can be stolen or its information duplicated by hackers and thieves. Therefore, more aggressive solutions are being pursued, including the handprint or facial recognition technology that identifies a person's unique vein patterns. More specificity means much less chance of duplication and theft. Your scanned hand information is securely stored in the cloud, along with your credit card and bank account information, and accessed by your browser or a particular retail website. And the chances of someone stealing or duplicating your unique epidermal information and vein patterns is virtually nil, to the point of being a nonexistent concern.

2. Personal Convenience

What if you never again had to carry a debit card with you? What if there was a more convenient way to make a payment or purchase an item? How great would that be? Simply place your groceries on the counter, pay for a meal, or buy some clothes by passing your hand over a scanner. And, like magic, your payment is complete and your purchase is immediately debited from your account. No more pulling out your wallet, fumbling through your purse, or worrying that someone might see you punch in your PIN.

3. Health Concerns

Because checks, bills, and coins are touched by thousands of human hands, they can easily spread and transmit infectious viruses. For this reason, cash may soon permanently be viewed as "dirty," potentially contaminated, or at the very least, antiquated.

4. Economic Unity and Uniformity

In ancient times, even before coins, bartering was a common means of buying and selling. We still see this practice today online, where people will trade one item for another. In 600 BC, King Aly-attes of Lydia (now western Turkey) created the first mint, and individual countries have since minted, printed, and circulated their own currencies.

On January 1, 1999, the euro was introduced to the world and was soon adopted by cooperating nations in the European Union. This marked a major step toward a universal currency.

Even more universal, however, are credit and debit cards. A person from any country in the world can travel just about anywhere and, with the swipe or insertion of a card, make a financial transaction. While the widespread use of cards has contributed to significant levels of global economic uniformity, it has been difficult to eliminate the many forms of theft and fraud that are connected to the use of plastic.

It remains to be seen whether this new biometric technology will gain the necessary traction for universal adoption in the immediate future. This does, however, clearly illustrate where the transaction industry is heading. Landlines died as cellphones were introduced. Then cell phones gave way to smartphones. Now we're seeing a similar streamlined trend within the world of economic transactions. And as more retail brick-and-mortar stores, along with online merchants, jockey to position themselves on the cutting edge of a competitive market, demand for efficient and secure procedures will no doubt increase.

As always, there are certain demographic groups of people who will be among the first to avail themselves of this futuristic financial transaction method. There is a process known as the *technology adoption lifecycle* that tracks the acceptance of a product into the mainstream. *Innovators* are the first group to make use of such products, followed by *early adapters*, the *early majority*, and the *late majority*. The last demographic is described as the *laggards* or *phobics,* who, due to apathy or resistance, finally have little choice but to capitulate to the majority. However, if another seismic health event, catastrophic disaster, or global financial crisis occurs, it could easily dictate a more rapid acceleration forward in transaction methods, one with which everyone would be required to comply.

Think about this: If a virus with a 97- to 99.75-percent recovery rate can move governments worldwide to mandate billions to wear masks, limit social contact, or stay home (all under the guiding principle of public health and safety and for the common good), then a cataclysmic global monetary implosion could do the same with regard to how we are permitted to buy and sell. And the message will be explicitly understood: Go along with the prescribed narrative, or face personal, economic, or legal consequences.

To illustrate: If, for alleged health reasons, cash transactions were suddenly no longer accepted in a particular store, you (the consumer) are logically forced to (1) make a digital or card transaction, (2) shop at another store, (3) stop buying that particular product altogether, or (4) do your shopping online. But what will happen when *all* grocery stores decide to discontinue *all* cash payments? Other than the unrealistic option of bartering with local farmers for meat, milk, and vegetables, your choices suddenly narrow dramatically. Or again, if some calamity forces (or fast-forwards) a necessity concerning how we purchase or sell, then we are *all* left with even fewer options. Some grocery stores are already experimenting with cashless, "checkout-free" options, installing cameras that read and scan your purchases as you remove them from aisle shelves.[9]

Realistically, where is all this heading? Where is it taking us? Do we have legitimate reason to be concerned, or is this simply a case of economic culture becoming more efficient? The answer is found in Reason 5.

5. Prophetic Fulfillment

What does all this have to do with Bible prophecy?

Well, *everything*, actually. As we've seen with globalism and government, what we're witnessing is a gradual transformation and shift of the human collective, one that is preparing us to welcome a single world leader. But in order to understand this prophesied reality more fully, we must step back and see the bigger picture.

The Bible tells us the coming Antichrist will receive his authority directly from the devil himself (Revelation 13:4). In other words, he will be 100 percent energized and possessed by Satan. Ever since his original rebellion, Satan has always longed to be worshipped as God (Isaiah 14:13-14). This unholy ambition is part of what has driven his attempt to author his own world history narrative through control of the nations (1 John 5:19).[10] As part of his strategy, Satan even attempted to persuade Jesus to bow down and worship him, offering the Son of God rulership over all the kingdoms of the world (Matthew 4:8-9). Interestingly, Jesus did not dispute the devil's ability to make such an offer. In fact, He later acknowledged Satan's preeminent position, even calling him the "ruler of this world" (John 12:31; 14:30; 16:11). The apostle Paul referred to him as the "god of this world" and the "prince of the power of the air" (2 Corinthians 4:4; Ephesians 2:2).

Today, it's abundantly clear to any believer possessing a morsel of biblical discernment that the devil is behind the official moral narrative and spirit of this age. And yet, for this evil entity who once aspired to heaven's throne, even this is not enough. Satan is obsessed with being exclusively worshipped, and every aspect of his global governmental strategy is designed toward this end. But because he exists as an angelic *spirit*, he must therefore assume or inhabit some physical form in order to be seen and to receive this worship. That's why it will be necessary for him to choose a man—the Antichrist.

Despite misguided speculation to the contrary, it is impossible for anyone to know who the Antichrist is right now, as his identity will not be revealed to humanity until after the rapture, when the restraining influence of the Holy Spirit through the church is removed (2 Thessalonians 2:6-7). But those with understanding during the tribulation *will* be able to pinpoint who the man of sin is (Revelation 13:18). Even so, there is still much the Bible has *already* revealed to us about him, thousands of years in advance of his diabolical debut.

All told, there are more than 100 passages in Scripture detailing Antichrist's origin, character, reign, deeds, and destiny. In fact, Scripture says more about this man than any other end-times person, with the exception of Jesus Himself. And though some have speculated Antichrist could even be a woman, we can be certain he will be a man, as the Bible repeatedly uses male pronouns to describe him (Daniel 8:23; 9:26; 2 Thessalonians 2:3-4).

This figure is given many names, each of them revealing specific aspects of his character and deeds. Of course, he is most known as "Antichrist," a term mentioned five times in the New Testament (1 John 2:18, 22; 4:3; 2 John 1:7). This tells us he is a real person and not merely representative of some wicked, rogue government or symbolic of an ethereal evil principle. The prophet Daniel, along with Zechariah, Jesus, Paul, and John portrays this man as a single individual and not a symbolic representation of something else (Daniel 7:18, 20, 24-25; 8:23, 25; 9:27; 11:21, 24, 31, 36-37; Zechariah 11:15-17; Matthew 24:15, 24; 2 Thessalonians 2:3-4, 8-9; 1 John 2:18-19, 22; 4:3; 2 John 1:7; Revelation 6:1-2; 13:1-18; 17:1-19; 19:19-20; 20:4).

That being established, some of Antichrist's specific names and titles include:

- the little horn (Daniel 7:8),
- the insolent king (Daniel 8:23),
- the prince who is to come (Daniel 9:26),
- the one who makes desolate (Daniel 9:27),
- the king who does as he pleases (Daniel 11:36),
- the man of lawlessness (2 Thessalonians 2:3),
- the son of destruction (2 Thessalonians 2:3),
- antichrist (1 John 2:18),
- the deceiver (2 John 1:7),
- the rider on a white horse (Revelation 6:2), and
- the beast (Revelation 13:1; used a total of 36 times in Revelation).

The Second Coming of Satan

From Scripture's composite portrait of him, we learn this individual will combine indescribable charm with unspeakable evil

(Daniel 7:8, 11, 25; 9:27; 11:36; Matthew 24:15; 2 Thessalonians 2:4, 7-12; Revelation 13:5). He will also be accompanied by a second beast, the false prophet, who will assist him, providing additional supernatural deception along with "power and signs and false wonders" (2 Thessalonians 2:9-10; see also Revelation 13:11-15). This global deception will include both actual signs and faux miracles so convincing that no one will be able to distinguish between the two. Scripture uses the same words to describe both Christ's *and* Antichrist's miracles, leading many to conclude that his display of the supernatural will undeniably be genuine. All that he does will be done to mimic the actual Christ, as the word *anti* not only means "against," but also "in place of." He will be the false messiah. The counterfeit Christ.

Of course, history has seen its share of devilish dictators, depraved despots, corrupt kings and rulers, serial killers, deceptive religious figures, and homicidal maniacs. But none have rivalled the heights of arrogance and the depths of moral decadence this man of sin will display. Compared to him, all who have come before are amateurs, mere shadows of his satanic substance.

He will truly be "the devil with skin on."

Exactly how does Antichrist fit into God's prophetic end-times narrative? What is his role? The Bible states that this man (most likely a Gentile) will arise in the final days to unite the world under a ten-nation confederation, one over which he himself will rule (Daniel 2:31-45; 7:19-28; Revelation 13:1-9). His kingdom, revealed from Daniel as a final form of the ancient Roman Empire, will rule over a regime embodying a trinity of political, religious, and economic branches (Daniel 9:27; 12:7; Revelation 13). He will arrive on history's shore bringing terms of peace, specifically to Israel (Daniel 9:27; Revelation 6:1-2). This historic covenant will be his first item of business and will not only establish him as a world leader, but also allow him to parlay a specific partnership with the Jews. The Antichrist's covenant with Israel, *not* the rapture, is what will officially begin the seven-year tribulation we see portrayed in Revelation chapters 6–19. The covenant will set in motion all the events prophesied thousands of years ago in Daniel and Revelation.

Antichrist's agenda will be global; therefore, the scope and power of his administration and actions must be as well. But while leading this international coalition of nations, something unexpected will occur three-and-a-half years into his reign. The Bible describes him as suffering a "fatal wound" (Revelation 13:2, 12, 14). The word used to picture his demise (slain) is the same word used to describe the death of Jesus the Lamb (Revelation 5:6) and refers to a violent, bloody death.

Scholars are divided as to whether this is an actual death or merely a grand, satanic ruse. Some argue that only God can bring a soul back from the afterlife. Others assert that during the seven-year tribulation the devil's leash will be long, and he will be allowed to perform signs and wonders not previously allowed by God. The phrase "it was given" is repeated throughout Revelation, indicating a special granting of authority from either God or Satan (Revelation 6:2, 4, 8; 7:2; 8:2; 9:1, 3, 5; 11:2, 3; 13:2, 4, 5, 14, 15; 20:4).

Antichrist is initially portrayed as "coming up out of the sea" (of Gentiles—Revelation 13:1; see also 17:15) to begin his seven-year reign. However, at the midpoint of the tribulation, this "beast" who "was and is not" (that is, was alive but now is dead) is seen as rising "up out of the *abyss*" (Revelation 11:7; 17:8). This "abyss" is traditionally portrayed as the abode of demons (Luke 8:21; Revelation 9:1-2, 11; 20:1, 3). Presumably, it is here, following his assassination, that Antichrist is fully indwelt and possessed by Satan—mind, body, and soul.

Regardless of whether the devil actually raises him from the dead or if this is the mother of all false miracles, Satan's end game will be achieved—the world will be convinced. Antichrist was dead and has come back to life, and thus will be viewed as divine (Revelation 13:3-4, 8, 12, 14-15).

This, then, is the ultimate delusion, and the greatest lie of all time (John 8:44; 2 Thessalonians 2:9-11). It is also *the* single supernatural sign that energizes Antichrist to enter the Jewish Temple, declaring himself to be God in what both Daniel and Jesus called the "abomination of desolation" (Daniel 9:27; 11:31; 12:11; Matthew 24:15; see also 2 Thessalonians 2:4). At this time, he will utter perhaps never-before-heard blasphemies against the God of heaven (2 Thessalonians 2:3-4; Revelation 13:5-6).

Satan's Seal

On the heels of his ascent to global godlike status, Antichrist, with the aid of the false prophet, will implement the full measure of his religious and economic doctrine as the two merge into one. Here is how Scripture describes it.

First, mandatory worship of Antichrist will be declared by law (Revelation 13:8-12). Most will comply willingly upon being convinced of his deity. Like most other satanic deceptions, the devil will find a way to make worshipping a political leader-turned-deity into an attractive prospect. And even though this worship is compulsory, it is still possible for people to resist and refuse, and many will—namely Jews and Christians. As a result, Antichrist will declare all-out war on them (Revelation 12:12-17; 13:7, 10). For those who are found and captured, the sentence will be swift and decisive—death by beheading. Here, John used a New Testament Greek word that refers to an ancient, barbaric method of execution (Revelation 6:9; 20:4). And just to ensure loyalty from the rest of humanity, a very specific mark will be required for all peoples, without which they are not allowed to buy or sell *anything* (Revelation 13:16-18).

No mark = no entry. No mark = no service. No mark = no sale— and no income.

Much has been written about the nature of this mark, including wild speculations of Antichrist obtaining "Satan's DNA" and somehow replicating it for distribution to the world, perhaps by synthesizing it into some sort of mandatory vaccine.[11]

Others wonder whether the mark will be an advanced form of personal identification tied to one's bank account (like Amazon's biometric scanning) an RFID (Radio Frequency Identification) chip, or perhaps a "smart tattoo." Though its exact nature or form is unclear, I believe we can draw some clear conclusions from Revelation's specificity.

First, the mark will be "on" (Greek, *epi*) not *in* the hand or forehead. This would appear to rule out any sort of chip or implant. Second, it stands to reason that this mark will also be visible. The Greek word John uses to describe the mark is *charagma*, which, in its first-century context, referred to an etching, engraving, or brand mark. This word was used to describe the facial image stamped on a coin or impressed into a seal. But it also came to be known as an identification marker used by slaveowners and by subordinate military officers wishing to identify themselves as being in subjection to a commanding officer. How apropos.

Given the nature and quality of life at the tribulation's midpoint (following the seal judgments), it is entirely conceivable that this mark could be considered *less* intrusive than previously envisioned. In other words, instead of some forced futuristic microchip implanted under the skin as many assume, something akin to a smart tattoo could be gladly welcomed and fulfill both purposes of Antichrist's mark.

Currently, smart tattoos are being tested by researchers at Harvard and MIT, primarily for medical purposes. The ink in the tattoo changes color to indicate an increase in glucose levels or an alert of dehydration. Curiously, their project has been named "Dermal *Abyss*."

Another version of the smart tattoo (again, *on* the skin, not underneath it) has been developed by Professor Yael Hanein of Tel Aviv University's Center for Nanoscience and Nanotechnology. This stick-on "nanotech tattoo" holds a "carbon electrode which can measure the activity of muscle and nerve cells."[12] The physiological data measured in muscles could also potentially track human emotions.

Other similar tattoo-like applications include:

- "Living tattoos"—These use genetically programmed living cells to respond to various internal or external stimuli.
- "Graphone tattoos"—These are ultrathin, wearable tattoos that conform to the skin, monitoring heart rate and other bodily responses.

These bio-wearable marks are also being tested in connection with smartphones and other wireless devices. They can be used as alternatives to typing in your PIN along with using facial or fingerprint recognition.[13]

Third, the mark of Antichrist will be the *only* means by which financial transactions can be made under the beast's regime. With digital tattoo technology presently either available or viably being tested, such a mark could be easily utilized as an economic passport, making the purchase and sale of goods much more streamlined and efficient.

Fourth, the mark will identify a person as a worshipper of the beast (Revelation 13:12, 15-17; 20:4). As such, those who receive this image or number will effectively seal their eternal destiny. According to Scripture, not one believer in Jesus will take the mark, and every person who does take it will end up in the eternal lake of fire (Revelation 19:20; see also 13:16-17; 16:2; 20:4).

Another possibility is that this mark may turn out to be even more primitive than any of the technologies described here. For a person to have the Antichrist's image or number on their hand or forehead (stamped, etched, tattooed) may merely grant that person *access* to buying and selling without actually facilitating the transaction itself in any way. In such a scenario, those who receive the mark would be free to use any preferred or allowed method of digital payment (cards, phones) or some form of biometric scanning (such as the one introduced by Amazon).

Those who argue for a more technologically sophisticated system associated with the mark believe it makes more sense for it to be a device that integrates both identity as well as financial information. And the current trajectory of technology would seem to point in that direction.

> The aftershocks we're experiencing at this time serve a dual purpose, also being foreshocks that indicate the soon emergence of the end of days.

Coming into Focus

No matter what the eventual nature, development, and implementation of the beast's mark, it will be *the* way in which Satan, via the false prophet and the Antichrist, will ensure that every living human "gives the devil his due," ascribing to him the glory and worship that he has craved these many thousands of years.

Fortunately for us, Scripture tells us exactly how the story ends for Satan, the Antichrist, and the false prophet (Revelation 19:20; 20:10). What we don't yet know is precisely *how* some of these prophecies will flesh out in their fulfillment. But with each prophetic foreshock we experience, Revelation's reality comes more into focus.

Current trends appear to predict an increasingly cashless society accompanied by a grooming of humanity to welcome a charismatic Messiah-like figure in the last days. This will be Satan's strategy to fulfill his deepest desires. With each passing year, we see unfolding before us the Bible's prophetic narrative. The things to come are truly on their way. The aftershocks we're experiencing at this time serve a dual purpose, also being foreshocks that indicate the soon emergence of the end of days.

Chapter 5

THE END-TIMES ECONOMIC COLLAPSE

In 1992, while a strategist for Bill Clinton's presidential campaign, James Carville coined a now-famous catchphrase that helped guide the Clinton team to victory in the election. The phrase? "It's the economy, stupid!" The savvy Carville was well aware that in order to persuade voters away from a sitting president who, just over a year earlier had enjoyed a 90 percent approval rating, he would have to zero in on what mattered most to the populace. He chose to focus on the economy—and Clinton went on to soundly beat George H.W. Bush.

An old adage states, "Money talks." It still does, and at times, it also *shouts*, particularly when the entire planet is experiencing an economic downturn. As much as we might wish it weren't the case, it's *always* about the money. Political platitudes may draw applause at campaign rallies, but policies that hit consumers in the wallet and bank account are what get people's attention—and their continued loyalty.

CLOSED

The global economic lunge brought on by the COVID scare of 2020 affected more than 200 countries, essentially the whole world.[1] Eighty countries went on to close their borders, ordering countless thousands of businesses to shut down (and due to financial losses, many will never reopen). Fifty million Americans filed for unemployment benefits, with 20 million losing their jobs. Small businesses went bankrupt at an unprecedented pace.[2]

This pushed the unemployment rate to 14.7 percent, historically the highest since the Great Depression of the 1930s.[3] The International Monetary Fund (IMF) then predicted massive unemployment for the global economy.[4] In European countries, 30 million applied for state support of wages, a blow to that region's economy unsurpassed in a peacetime era. Some 1.5 billion children were suddenly out of school worldwide. The domino effect of these shutdowns caused unemployment rates to continue skyrocketing, further driving the fiscal fallout, triggering rising levels of poverty, financial hardship, interrupted lives, and careers derailed. This mass misfortune was mixed in with a hornet's nest of social unrest. In Minneapolis alone, more than 500 million dollars in damage was done by rioting mobs protesting what they saw as racial injustice. Eventually, the National Guard was called in to help restore order.

As a second wave of the virus threatened, experts began predicting global trade could fall by as much as 32 percent. It was impossible for even the most informed medical or pandemic professionals to be certain whether this trend would peak, or if successive waves would continue rippling well into the future. As time went on, serious questions arose about the validity of the statistics measuring the numbers of the infected and dead, which appeared to be contaminated with inaccurate data and misinformation, even from the Centers for Disease Control.[5]

Even so, perception oftentimes *is* reality, prompting the European Commission to declare the pandemic a national health and security issue, as well as a "national economic priority" on the same level as terrorism, cyberattacks, and weapons of mass destruction.[6]

Further economic earthquakes were felt in international trade, tourism, the medical supply industry, consumer electronics, and financial markets. The IMF, along with the World Bank, forecasted a weak financial future moving forward. Leaders across the globe were left scratching their heads, wondering where all this would take us and what the long-term impact on 7.8 billion people would be.

"But wait a minute," you may say. "Haven't we survived serious economic recessions and declines before? Why should we be so concerned about this one? What makes this 'Great Lockdown' so unique?" To start, we don't yet fully comprehend the long-term effects of business closings, international trade interruptions, prolonged unemployment, global supply chain disruptions, and even social distancing, which makes a reasonable financial prognosis nearly impossible. This leads many experts to appeal to another age-old adage: "Hope for the best, but prepare for the worst."

Yes, hope. That comforting feeling of believing everything will turn out all right in the end. But will it? Was 2020 merely an unpleasant economic blip on the global radar, or a harbinger of things to come? Will America and the rest of the world be able to sift through the rubble and somehow find ways to rebuild and recoup all that was lost? Or is that even possible? Will social unrest, rioting, anarchy, and violence become the new normal under state governments that allowed significant portions of major cities to fall to lawless mobs? How many years will it take to bounce back to a robust economy? Or assuming we are able to restore a semblance of our former economic stability, what damage will have been done? What permanent economic scars will hinder that progress? Will humanity experience an enduring "collective PTSD" over all this, especially in an age where the human psyche seems to be weaker than that of previous generations?

Wake Up or Wipe Out?

You could argue that the unforeseen COVID pandemic served as a wake-up call, revealing our unpreparedness for such a far-reaching crisis. As such, it may prove to be a new generation's version of Pearl Harbor or 9/11, with ripple effects reaching virtually every pocket of society. A watershed phenomenon, in many ways COVID-19 forever altered our lifestyles, marking our cumulative consciousness like a brand.

But the question remains: Can we ever go back to the way it was? Or will this global crisis reshape and redefine us, preventing us from ever recapturing the peace and prosperity of former days?

Have we reached a point of no return?

Financial experts have a term for what we've been experiencing. They're called black-swan events and are defined as "an event in human history that was unprecedented and unexpected at the point in time it occurred."[7] The term comes from the largely Western belief that swans are white. Therefore, a black swan is considered an anomaly in the species.

I think it's safe to say that 2020 was a black-swan *year*.

Just when another such "unexpected, unprecedented" event comparable to the COVID phenomenon will occur is unknown. But like the black swans themselves, we know they're out there. They just haven't appeared yet. And, according to the World Economic Forum, this is exactly what fuels a subterranean, planetwide fear concerning global risks, including the threat of

- nuclear war
- conventional war

- war in the Middle East
- widespread famine
- ecological disasters
- pandemics and contagions
- governmental tyranny
- natural disasters
- catastrophic climate change
- some cosmic extinction event
- and yes, global financial collapse[8]

These are all real and very potential threats. And according to the Bible, virtually all of them are a part of planet Earth's future, including a much more severe and comprehensive season of economic devastation.

Riders on the Storm

The seal judgments in Revelation 6 inaugurate the first wave of God's catastrophic judgments on this world during the tribulation period. Known as the seven seal judgments, they picture the unfolding of successive related events that will shake both the world and its inhabitants. The first series of seal judgments involves the infamous four horsemen of the apocalypse. John writes that from among the four living creatures a "voice of thunder" summons with a single word, "come" (verse 1). Immediately upon Earth's stage appears a white horse, "and he who sat upon it had a bow; and a crown was given to him; and he went out conquering and to conquer" (verse 2).

Some have interpreted this rider to be Jesus, but the passage, along with the rest of Revelation, does not appear to support such a view. Christ is the one breaking the seals, not mounting a horse in response to the breaking of those seals. Also, this rider wears only one crown (Greek, *stephanos* = "wreath of victory"), whereas Christ, in Revelation 19:12, is adorned with "many diadems" (that is, royal crowns). The rider in Revelation 6 carries an arrowless bow, but in chapter 19, Jesus wields a sword. This rider in Revelation 6 brings peace to the earth, while the authentic Christ will bring wrath at His coming. Further, Jesus will not return to the earth until the end of the seven-year season of judgment, not at the beginning.

Undoubtedly then, this rider is the Antichrist, arriving on the world scene bringing a powerful message of peace. In the early hours following the rapture, people will see "an outbreak of deception and counterfeit Christs who will claim to have the answers for the world's chaos. Eventually, one man will quickly stand out head and shoulders above the rest. He will be the decisive fulfillment of the rider on the white horse—the ultimate anti-Messiah. We know him best as the Antichrist."[9] Dr. David Jeremiah designates him as a "Dark Prince on a White Horse."[10]

Scholars and commentators make special note in observing that this rider possesses a bow, but no arrows. This signifies his ability to conquer without the use of military might. Like the one he mimics, his word is also his weapon—at least initially. A skilled and mighty orator, this false Christ will woo the nations with his silver tongue of persuasion (Daniel 7:8, 11; 11:36; 13:5). Therefore, his will be a bloodless victory. He will achieve peace through ink rather than blood. And the world will adore him for it. No doubt the Nobel Peace Prize will be awarded to him. But this phenomenon is not without precedent, for during difficult times, humanity inherently longs for a savior-figure.

On November 21, 1922, the following appeared in *The New York Times* concerning the newly elected chancellor of Germany: "He exerts an uncanny control over audiences, possessing the remarkable ability to not only rouse his hearers to a fighting pitch of fury, but at will turn right around and reduce the same audience to docile coolness."[11]

And Germany swooned.

Eighty-six years later, and on a different continent, Barack Obama stood before a watching world, self-proclaiming his Democratic party's nomination would be remembered as "the moment when the rise of the oceans began to slow and our planet began to heal."[12]

And America swooned.

I wonder what will be said of Antichrist upon his ascent to the pinnacle of peace and world leadership. What accolades and adulation will be heaped upon him? What will the media write and say about his ability to influence and romance a global audience with his speech, persona, and presentation?

While the world will be swept away by an unprecedented sense of hope and security by the Antichrist, his golden age of peace will be short-lived. It is on the very heels of this peace that a second horse and rider appear and are also bid, "Come." This time we see a red horse, and the rider on it "was granted to take peace from the earth, and that men would slay one another; and a great sword was given to him" (6:4).

There are several points we can unpack from this verse. First, the horse's color is red, which, in context, indicates widespread bloodshed.[13] Second, the rider is most likely representative of the many military forces or nations involved in a global conflict. We aren't told which nations, but the economic destruction and loss of life that results from this war is unmistakable. Third, while this rider will "take" peace from the earth, Israel will remain under the protection of the peace accord established by the first rider (Daniel 7:25; 9:27; 12:7). This peace agreement will last for 42 months. But for a significant portion of the rest of the world (as we will soon see), bloodshed and death are their portion. This prophecy retroactively illustrates the restraining power of God during our current (church) age. Whoever these warring forces may be, they are presently being prevented from engaging in this massive conflict *until* the appointed future time.

The result of this coming war is that people will "*slay* one another." John here used the same word he employed to describe the violent deaths of Christ, Antichrist, and the tribulation martyrs (Revelation 5:6, 9, 12; 6:4, 9; 13:3, 8; 18:24). In other words, the killing will be very violent.

The Greek word translated "sword" here is a word that typically referred to a short, dagger-like knife, like the one used by Peter in the Garden of Gethsemane (John 18:10). But in Scripture, a sword (Greek, *machaira*) can also be the long sword of a Roman soldier in battle, or the kind that was used by Rome to inflict capital punishment (Romans 8:35; 13:4). The one pictured here is also "great" (Greek, *mega*), meaning its use results in a great loss of life.

As it turns out, Spanish-American philosopher George Santayana was right when he wrote, "Only the dead have seen the end of war."[14]

War is the ultimate agent of death, a fact corroborated by history.

An estimated 37,000 lost their lives in the Revolutionary War for America's independence. The Napoleonic wars saw between 3.5 to 7 million dead. America's Civil War was responsible for taking between 600,000 to 1 million lives. For World War I, the toll was 17 to 50 million (including those who died from the Spanish flu epidemic). World War II saw 55 to 85 million lives taken from 1939-1945. Since that time, more than 60 major regional and international conflicts have occurred, with a cumulative death toll of more than 40 million.

Admittedly, the past has not been peaceful. But neither will the future be. However, the international conflict we see prophesied in Revelation 6 will dwarf all the previous wars in history, perhaps with the aid of multiple nuclear deployments.

Daily Bread and a Denarius

Because of the massive death toll brought on by this tribulation-era war, the event cannot be applied to any other previous military conflict in history, thus confirming it is a still-future event. And the aftershocks will be global in their reach.

With the third seal judgment we see the arrival of the next horse: "I looked, and behold, a black horse; and he who sat on it had a pair of scales in his hand. And I heard something like a voice in the center of the four living creatures saying, 'A quart of wheat for a denarius, and three quarts of barley for a denarius; and do not damage the oil and the wine'" (6:5-6).

Each of these "four living creatures" before God's throne are of the cherubim class of angelic beings. In Revelation 4, John described them as "full of eyes in front and behind," resembling respectively a lion, a calf, the face of a man, and "like a flying eagle" (verses 6-7). They also possess six wings and incessantly proclaim God's transcendence, eternality, and holy nature (Revelation 4:6-9; see also Psalm 89:1; 99:1; Ezekiel 1:1-25; 10:15, 20; 28:14, 16). One by one, these four living creatures are tasked with calling forth the apocalyptic horses and their riders.

Again, the third horse is black, a color which, since antiquity, has been associated with sorrow and lamentation. The immediate context here supports that connection. Great sorrow follows great war. And the direct consequence of international conflict is widespread famine. At the close of World War II, 20 to 25 million people had perished due to starvation or hunger-related diseases. In the United

States and Great Britain, food was rationed to prevent the threat of epidemic starvation. Food shortages are a common component of every major war, and during desperate, critical times, humans will cheat, lie, steal, and even kill just to secure a morsel of bread. During the Babylonian siege of Jerusalem in 586 BC, the food shortage and famine was so severe that mothers boiled their own infants and ate them (Lamentation 2:20; 4:8-10)!

With the arrival of the black horse and its rider, famine will spread like a wild brushfire, affecting billions. How desperate will people be in a world where the Holy Spirit's restraining influence has been removed?

John notes that the rider on the black horse holds a pair of scales in his hand.[15] Here, a mysterious voice announcing this future famine comes from "the center of the four living creatures"—that is, the throne in their midst. Most scholars conclude the voice is that of Jesus or the Father. Because Christ is the one who instigates the seal judgments, it could well be His voice, though in times past, God the Father has also decreed famine (2 Kings 8:1; Jeremiah 16:4; Haggai 1:11; 2:16-17). In any case, the need to measure food by weight here is an indication of the severity of this famine. A "measure" of wheat is slightly less than a quart (in dry measure). Wheat was the basic staple of John's first-century world, and a "measure" was just enough to sustain one person for one day. A denarius (Roman silver coin) was an average day's wage. Therefore, "a quart of wheat for a denarius" means that an entire day's labor will be required just to produce enough for a person to survive for one day. To put this in perspective, ordinarily a denarius would buy 8 quarts of wheat or 24 quarts of barley, which was cheaper but also less nutritious. Calculations reveal that the inflation following this tribulation-era war will soar to 800 percent! Famine and poverty will rise to all-time historic highs.

Interestingly, the divine voice here forbids this war, famine, and economic inflation to "damage the oil and the wine" (6:6).[16] Oil and wine were considered luxuries, especially compared to wheat and barley, and were mostly associated with the wealthy. Therefore, those with greater financial resources at the time of this judgment will not be as affected by runaway inflation and food shortages as most others will. This is true about today's financial crises as well—the rich are, on the whole, more insulated from disasters due to their resources and reserves.

In summary, this massive economic earthquake, brought on by war and resulting in famine, will affect the common people vastly more than those with abundant wealth. The luxurious lifestyles of the rich and famous (or at least their dinner tables) will continue relatively untouched throughout the third seal judgment. That tells us today's liberal perception of economic injustice will continue into the beginning stages of the tribulation.

The Grim Reaper and the Grave Digger

Lest we conclude that God somehow favors the rich here, what we see take place during this judgment is simply the natural and historical differences implicit between economic classes. And the ease of the rich will not last long. Though relatively unaffected here, we are told that "the rich and the strong" will suffer horribly during the sixth seal judgment, along with everyone else (6:12-17).

To date, no war, famine, or economic devastation has ever ravaged planet Earth and obliterated humanity like the one prophesied here. The extent of this devastation is without equal. And it will get even worse when the fourth horse arrives.

"I looked, and behold, an ashen horse; and he who sat on it had the name Death; and Hades was following with him. And authority was given to them over a fourth of the earth, to kill with sword and with famine and with pestilence and by the wild beasts of the earth" (6:8).

The fourth living creature speaks, and a final horse and rider appear. This horse is a pallor green, or pale, sickly, ashen green. The word translated "ashen" (Greek, *chloros*) pictures a corpse in a state of decay. Mounted upon this pale horse is death personified. And Hades (the place of the dead) is following closely on his heels. Bible teacher Chuck Swindoll names them the "Grim Reaper and the Grave Digger."[17]

And the final body count from these apocalyptic horsemen? A staggering *one-fourth* of Earth's population. This number is almost unimaginable. If such judgments were to occur in our present day, close to two billion people would be dead.[18]

John carefully categorizes the causes of death here for us: the sword of war (violent deaths), famine (hopeless deaths), pestilence (painful deaths), and "wild beasts of the earth" (terrifying deaths). We've talked about war and famine, which are closely tied to economic collapse. But what about the other two?

The word translated "pestilence" is the same word John uses for "death" earlier in the verse. This word is used in Revelation 2:23 to refer to a contagion or deadly disease. When interviewed by *The Washington Post* in March of 2020, I categorically stated that the coronavirus was *not* the fulfillment of the prophesied fourth seal judgment we see in Revelation 6.[19]

However, what the 2020 pandemic *did* demonstrate is how quickly a virus can spread in our modern world, and how weak and vulnerable humanity and the economy really are. As it relates to future prophecy, the virus was merely a foretaste of things much more devastating to come.

The Greek term John uses for "wild beasts" is *therion*, which refs to a ravenous beast or animal. This has been interpreted as referring to the Antichrist and false prophet, both of whom are described by this same word in Revelation a total of 38 times. And from a purely grammatical standpoint, this verse would appear to justify that interpretation. However, I believe it is too early in the tribulation for the false prophet to begin murdering millions. His rampage doesn't officially begin until the midpoint of the seven-year period.

Another view suggests *therion* describes literal wild animals, who, due to lack of food and the trauma of being exposed to weapons of mass destruction, become ravenous and attack humans. A third view sees "wild beasts" as animals who carry infectious disease (like rats, birds, bats, racoons, dogs, etc.). Currently, there are more than 100 diseases that can be spread from animals to humans.[20] According to this view, an untold number of animal species will contract a wide variety of deadly diseases, spreading them to humans through rabid-like attacks and contributing to the high mortality rate (this could be why they are linked with pestilence in this passage).

Regardless of how the pestilence is caused or spread, the fact remains: More than one billion people will suffer brutal deaths, every one of them directly stemming from the wrath "of Him who sits on the throne, and from the wrath of the Lamb" (6:16-17). Truly, the great day of God's fury will begin with the seal judgments.

It will be the greatest single loss of life since Noah's flood (Genesis 6–9).[21]

Prophetic Parallels

However, John's Revelation prophecy was not the first time the earliest Christians heard about the calamities to come. During the last week of His life, Jesus took His disciples to the Mount of Olives, and there, they asked Him, "Tell us, when these things will happen, and what will be the sign of Your coming, and of the end of the age?" (Matthew 24:3).

Jesus had earlier prophesied regarding the total destruction of the Jewish Temple (verse 2). Then in response to the disciples' question, He walked them through the apocalyptic narrative we read about in Revelation 6–7. In fact, the parallels between Jesus' Olivet discourse and Revelation are unmistakable.

Matthew 24:4-14; Luke 21:7-13	Revelation 6–7
False Christs (verses 4-5)	Rider on the white horse (verses 1-2)
Wars and rumors of wars (verses 6-7)	Rider on the red horse (verses 3-4)
Famines and earthquakes (verse 7)	Rider on the black horse (verses 5-6)
Plagues and famines (verse 7; Luke 21:11)	Rider on the ashen horse (verses 7-8)
Persecution/martyrdom (verses 9-10)	Martyrs (verses 9-11)
Terrors and signs in the sky (Luke 21:11)	Terrors and signs in the sky (verses 12-17)
Gospel preached to the whole world (24:14)	144,000 Jewish evangelists (7:1-8)

Dr. Luke includes supplemental details about the same mountaintop sermon, adding Jesus' words, "When you hear of wars and disturbances, do not be terrified; for these things must take place first, but the end does not follow immediately" (21:9).

Jesus then continues His prophetic revelation, saying, "Nation will rise against nation and kingdom against kingdom, and there will be great earthquakes, and in various places *plagues* and *famines*, and there will be terrors and great signs from heaven" (Luke 21:9-11).

> With every foreshadowing disaster we experience
> in our day, the rumblings of approaching
> hoofbeats grow louder on the horizon.

Mark covers the same topic and includes Jesus' word about famine (Mark 13:8). Both Matthew and Mark quote Jesus as prophesying that this period (the first half of the tribulation) is "merely the beginning of birth pangs" (Matthew 24:8; Mark 13:8). Any woman who has borne a child understands the trauma of birth contractions.

Seven hundred years earlier, Isaiah also prophesied about this future time of judgment, writing,

> They will be terrified,
>> Pains and anguish will take hold of them;
>> They will writhe like a woman in labor,
> They will look at one another in astonishment,
>> Their faces aflame.
> Behold, the day of the LORD is coming,
>> Cruel, with fury and burning anger,
> To make the land a desolation;
>> And He will exterminate its sinners from it (13:8-9).

The apostle Paul adds his own amen, writing to the Thessalonians, "While they are saying, 'Peace and safety!' then destruction will come upon them suddenly like labor pains upon a woman with child, and they will not escape" (1 Thessalonians 5:3).

As with actual birth contractions, these "pains" will not only grow in intensity but also frequency as the day of Jesus' return draws nearer.

Turning to our day, the economic challenges and downturns we have experienced are hardly worthy to be mentioned in the same sentence with what is coming during the time of tribulation.

God's seal judgments will trigger a massive upheaval that reverberates throughout the world—with war, economic collapse, famine, and pestilence contributing to one-fourth of humanity being summoned to the grave. And this is just the introduction to Revelation's wrath!

In the end, despite every effort made to prevent a global financial meltdown and to preserve world peace, catastrophes and calamities are coming. The United Nations will not save us. Neither will international summits promoting economic unity or global forums convened to prevent climate change. All of them will prove futile as God Himself brings these future judgments upon a rebellious and wicked planet. And with every foreshadowing disaster we experience in our day, the rumblings of approaching hoofbeats grow louder on the horizon. Could the four horsemen of Revelation 6 be saddling up even now, preparing to ride and deliver these seal judgments into history's arena?

Chapter 6

ISRAEL AND THE RISE OF ANTISEMITISM

On November 7, 1938, 17-year old Herschel Grynszpan spent 245 francs on a revolver and a box of bullets, snuck it into the German embassy in Paris, and fatally shot 29-year-old Ernst vom Rath, an embassy official. Grynszpan had approached the reception desk, asking to speak to an official about a secret document he believed was of high value and interest to Germany. When asked by vom Rath for the supposed document, the teenager reportedly replied, "In the name of twelve thousand persecuted Jews, here is the document!" He then emptied all five shots from the handgun, hitting vom Rath twice in the abdomen.

Himself a refugee from Germany, Grynszpan had been distraught upon hearing his native country had expelled his family and was force-marching them to a refugee camp in Poland. Arrested on the spot, officials discovered the price tag still hanging on the revolver's trigger.

Two days later, Ernst vom Rath died, igniting a hellstorm of vengeance on Jews in Germany, which eventually culminated in the Holocaust.

Defeated, Scattered, and Misunderstood

In AD 70, Vespasian was proclaimed Rome's emperor following the death of Nero and a subsequent power struggle. One of the problems Vespasian inherited was a Jewish rebellion that had been going on in Judea for some four years. Once he quelled the greater part of this rebellion, he turned his attention toward the city of Jerusalem, where many Jews had fortified themselves.

Four years earlier, then-General Vespasian had begun the job of crushing the Jewish insurrection. Now, as emperor, one of his first actions was to commission his son, Titus, now himself a general, to finish the job. After a four-month siege, Titus sacked Jerusalem in AD 70. During the siege, many of the Jews inside the city walls died of starvation. The temple was burned down (with Jews trapped within), and tens of thousands were slaughtered, while the survivors were sold into slavery.[1] This historic siege effectively ended the Jewish state and began the diaspora, or the scattering of the Hebrew people across the world. And they would remain dispersed in more than 70 nations for the next 2,000 years (Deuteronomy 28:63-67). The Jewish people would find themselves strangers in strange lands. And sadly, persecution followed them wherever they went.

However, after the fall of Jerusalem, and during the subsequent era of the early church fathers, many respected Christian leaders failed to understand God's covenantal relationship with Israel, thus misrepresenting the role of the Jews in Scripture. A large number of them viewed the *church* as Israel's replacement, asserting that the promises originally made to the Jewish nation were always intended for the church.[2] Tertullian (AD 160–220) even wrote a work entitled "Against the Jews." Origen of Alexandria (AD 185–254), in his work *Contra Celsus*, is said to have promoted the idea of Jews as "Christ killers."

John Chrysostom (AD 344–407) called the Jewish synagogue "worse than a brothel…a den of scoundrels…temple of demons… a place of meeting for the assassins of Christ…I hate the synagogue…I hate the Jews."[3] From Augustine (who contended that the Jews deserved death) through to the Reformation (Martin Luther, who called the Jews "a miserable and accursed people…stupid fools…the great vermin of humanity"[4]), this spirit of antisemitism continued to brew. This perpetual disdain can be traced to roughly four sources:

1. A faulty approach to Scripture concerning some areas of theology. Many of the church fathers adhered to a symbolic or allegorical approach to interpretation, leading them to conclude that Israel served as an allegory pointing to deeper truth (that is, Jesus' planned relationship with His church).

2. An inability to understand the unconditional promises made by God to Israel (Genesis 12:3).

3. An inability to understand the "partial hardening" God had placed upon the Jews, and why they refused to renounce Judaism and turn to Jesus (Romans 11:25-26).

4. A lack of love for the Jewish people (Romans 9:1-5).

"Blame the Jews."

It's an oft-repeated refrain from throughout the past 2,000 years. During the Middle Ages, the Jewish people were blamed for everything from the bubonic plague to what was called blood libel, or kidnapping and murdering the children of Christians so they could use their blood in Jewish rituals. Olivier J. Melnick, in his excellent book *End-Times Antisemitism*, notes that "over 150 claims of blood libel were recorded throughout history resulting in the deaths of Jewish people."[5] Whole villages were wiped out, with many Jews drowned. As fallout from the Crusades, they were slaughtered under the slogan "Kill a Jew, save your soul!"

Under the reign of the Catholic Church's papacy in 1215, the Church adopted the doctrine of transubstantiation, or the belief that the wafer and wine actually become the body and blood of Jesus during communion. Roughly 30 years later, in the town of Belitz, Germany, every Jewish person living there was murdered. The justification? They were accused of "desecrating the host." In reality, what had happened was that mold (*Micrococcus prodigiosus*, or what has come to be known as "bleeding bread") had grown on the bread used for Catholic communion, giving it the appearance of blood. And who could be held responsible for such a desecration *except* the infidel Jews? All told, more than 100,000 Jews were slaughtered in some 140 communities.

In 1321, Jews in Tunisia were accused of poisoning wells in an effort to wipe out Christians. In retaliation, 5,000 Jews were killed.

As mentioned earlier, Jews were also blamed for Black Death, or the bubonic plague (1346–1353), which killed 25 million worldwide, wiping out somewhere between 20 to 60 percent of Europe's population.

Dragged from their homes, Jewish families were cast alive into public bonfires, had their property confiscated, or were thrown in jail. As a result of this persecution, large numbers of Hebrews began migrating to neighboring European countries, populating those areas to this day.

But as everyone knows, the Jews were *not* responsible for the bubonic plague. Instead, the reason for their unusually low sickness and mortality rates during the plague years is explained by their refusal to drink from public fountains because of their faith, not because they secretly poisoned people. They practiced strict, religious dietary laws and cleansing rituals that essentially disinfected them. They also typically lived in their own communities, shielding them from general exposure to the deadly disease.

The Final Solution

Fast-forward to 1933. Adolf Hitler became the chancellor of Nazi Germany. He believed the German people were part of a superior Aryan race, and that Jews were a Semitic subrace. During this time, the Jewish populace in Germany was blamed as the cause of virtually every problem in the nation, from contributing to that country's loss in World War I to the decline in the German economy. Hitler thus began the systematic removal of Jews from German culture. Jewish books were banned, collected, and burned. A yellow Star of David was required to be worn on the lapel of all Jews and even those who were alleged to be Jewish—even if only one grandparent was Jewish. As a result, tens of thousands of Jews began emigrating out of Germany, seeking refuge in Western European countries and the United States. Albert Einstein was one of them. Eventually, Germany's aggression in war would close all avenues of escape for the Jews.

It didn't take long for things to take a terrible turn for the worse. Public sentiment rose to the point of outright hostility against Abraham's seed. Joseph Goebbels, head of the Nazi Ministry of Public Enlightenment and Propaganda, boasted, "A Jew is for me an object of disgust. I feel like vomiting when I see one. Christ could not possibly have been a Jew. It is not necessary to prove that scientifically—it is a fact. I do not need to prove this with science or scholarship. It is so!"[6]

In his book *Mein Kampf*, Hitler compared "filthy Jews" to "maggots."[7]

Then came November 9, 1938, the evening known as *Kristall-nacht*, or "Night of Broken Glass." Under the guise of enacting revenge for Herschel Grynzspan's murder of German diplomatic Ernst vom Rath in Paris, a coordinated rampage against Jews was executed throughout Germany, Austria, and Czechoslovakia. Hitler's stormtroopers (Sturmabteiling, known as "Brownshirts") ransacked some 7,500 businesses, breaking windows and destroying and looting many stores. They, along with German civilians, rounded up 30,000 Jewish males who were eventually sent to concentration camps. They also robbed 1,600 synagogues, with some 300 set ablaze to burn into the night.

The Nazis then forced Jews to pay for the costs of these raids, even confiscating insurance monies from the damages and compelling Jewish store owners to cover the expenses needed to repair their own buildings. The Nazis also added a 20 percent "atonement fee" on all German businesses owned by Jews, totaling 1 billion Reichsmarks.

In Hitler's regime, the Jews clearly were the "problem" for which a "solution" was needed. Following *Kristallnacht* came the Einsatzgruppen (SS death squads), which rounded up Jews for execution by firing squads. But this soon proved inefficient, as it would take too long to accomplish their ultimate goal of exterminating 11 million European Jews. Gas trucks were then introduced, but they, too, proved too slow for the impatient Nazis.

Meanwhile, tens of thousands of Jewish people were herded into ghettos in their respective towns, forced to live in overcrowded, substandard conditions. While there, they unknowingly waited to board cattle cars that would transport them to their final destinations—the labor and death camps that became the favored strategy for accomplishing Hitler's grisly objective.

Twenty main camps were constructed, with names that even

today send a mixed chill of horror, sorrow, and unbelief down the spine: among them Auschwitz, Dachau, Treblinka, Sobibor, Belzec, Bergen-Belsen, Buchenwald, and Ravensbrück. The hard labor in these camps was cruel and appalling enough. However, not satisfied with simply enslaving and killing these "undesirables," Hitler's demented doctors also performed unspeakable and depraved medical experiments on their subjects, using them as human lab rats in "research" that often resulted in their death. All these actions were vital components of Hitler's Final Solution.

Israel Reborn…to Trouble

After the fall of Germany's Third Reich and the liberation of Europe, a global outpouring of sympathy contributed to Israel being recognized as a state on May 14 (which happens to be my birthday). Eleven minutes following this declaration, President Harry S. Truman issued a statement recognizing "the provisional Jewish government as the de facto authority of the new State of Israel."[8]

The *very next day*, five Arab nations invaded Israel, and the nine-month Arab-Israeli War began.[9] Many more wars and skirmishes would follow in subsequent decades.

But apart from military conflicts, individual attacks on Israel and the Jewish people (simply *because* they are Jews) continue to this day. With mobs chanting "death to Israel" and other calls for Jewish extermination, Israel's Muslim neighbors are determined to wipe her off the map, vowing to finish the job Hitler started.[10]

Today, the Anti-Defamation League (ADL) keeps track of antisemitic attitudes and incidents worldwide. In a survey conducted in more than 100 countries, the league found that more than 1 *billion* people in the world harbor antisemitic attitudes.[11] They also discovered that "35 percent of people in the countries polled had never heard of the Holocaust, and 74 percent of people in the Middle East and North Africa hold anti-Semitic attitudes." According to the ADL, in 2019 alone there were 2,107 incidents of antisemitism recorded globally—ranging in everything from vandalism, assault, and shootings—an increase of 12 percent from the year before, and the highest since 1979.[12]

The nation of Israel has been called everything from a "cancer" that must be removed to a "filthy, infectious microbe" and that she must be "erased from the page of time."[13]

According to NBC News, violence against Jews in America is on the uptick.[14] And a resurgence of Jewish hatred has arisen in Europe. According to *The Atlantic*,

> France's 475,000 Jews represent less than 1 percent of the country's population. Yet last year, according to the French Interior Ministry, 51 percent of all racist attacks targeted Jews. The statistics in other countries, including Great Britain, are similarly dismal. In 2014, Jews in Europe were murdered, raped, beaten, stalked, chased, harassed, spat on, and insulted for being Jewish. *Sale Juif*—"dirty Jew"— rang in the streets, as did "Death to the Jews," and "Jews to the gas."[15]

This is a textbook example of modern racism. Ironically, this persecution is part of what's fueling the *Aliyah* (Hebrew = "ascent, or going up, immigrating to their ancestral home"). Once again, persecution is helping to build a stronger Israel.

More recently, a study at Oxford University found that 19.1 percent of the public in Britain believe to some degree that Jews caused the coronavirus pandemic.[16]

Seriously?

There are some who have put forth the idea that Jews created the virus to collapse the British economy and then to profit from the collapse. Such theories are, of course, absurd. And yet that anyone would believe such foolishness speaks to an underlying animosity against the Jewish people.

Following suit, the Palestinian Authority accused Israel of deliberately spreading the virus in Palestinian territories.[17] Even the tragic 2020 death of a black man, George Floyd, which sparked social unrest across the United States, was seized upon by antisemites to blame the Jews. These antisemites claimed that kneeling on a victim's neck was a technique taught by Israel Defense Forces to America's police forces.[18] And various extremist groups here in the United States, along with the Democratic party, take an unapologetic anti-Israel stance, with outspoken Muslim congresswomen joining in the rant.

Blame the Jews.

All through the ages, the Jewish people have been a lightning rod, drawing fire and criticism for unsubstantiated and unmerited reasons. It's the same spirit exhibited in the nations that once conspired against ancient Israel, saying, "Come, and let us wipe them out as a nation, that the name of Israel may be remembered no more" (Psalm 83:4).

No one can deny that discrimination, prejudice, and racism exist. Jesus made it very clear that all these types of "evil thoughts" (Mark 7:21-23) have their genesis in the heart of man, which is "more deceitful than all else and desperately sick" (Jeremiah 17:9). And yet despite all the charges and cries of injustice by minorities and marginalized identity groups, no people group throughout history can say they have suffered similar levels of hatred, demonization, abuse, discrimination, and attempted extermination that the Jewish people have faced.

Getting to the Heart of the Hatred

So, where did all this hatred begin? And where is it headed? Though experts outwardly trace this spirit of hate to right-wing supremacists, extreme-left liberal ideologies, and violent Islamic radicals, could there be a deeper and perhaps *unseen* cause?

The Bible says there is.

To solve this mystery, we must trace the clues all the way back to the beginning. That's where the Bible provides us some "declassified intel." It is reasonable to conclude that such hatred for a single people group cannot be fully explained in the physical realm, but rather, must have spiritual and supernatural origins. In Scripture's first book, we read, "I will put enmity between you and the woman, and between your seed and her seed; he [her seed] shall bruise you on the head, and you shall bruise him on the heel" (Genesis 3:15).

Here, God pronounced the curse on the satanically indwelt serpent, who, prior to this, had deceived and tempted Adam and Eve, resulting in humanity's plunge into sin. Besides prophesying Satan's ultimate doom, God also made it clear that there would be hostility, animosity, and conflict between the serpent's children and the offspring of the woman (John 8:44; 10:10; 1 Peter 5:8; Revelation 12:4, 9; 20:2). This verse saw its ultimate fulfillment in Christ and His victorious work on the cross. It is there that the devil's defeat was secured (John 16:11; 1 John 3:8).

Genesis 3:15 highlights the reason for Satan's hatred of the Jewish people. It was through a Jewish woman (Mary) and Jewish lineage that the Messiah was eventually born. Incidentally, Satan never knew which virgin would bear the Messiah, or when His birth would take place, so he was ready and waiting when Christ was born.

We can trace Satan's hatred of the Jewish people all the way back to Genesis, to the very beginning. He has always hated the Jews. Of course, he despises all people, no matter what their race or ethnic origin, because every person was created in the image of God (Genesis 1:26). Satan hated the first man, Adam, who was given coregent status over creation and the animal kingdom (Genesis 1:26; 2:20; Psalm 8:6-8). But for the Jew, Satan has reserved a special level of contempt and animosity.

Genesis 12:3 is another reason for Satan to hate the Hebrews. Here, God promised Abraham (the patriarch of the Jewish people) that "in you all the families of the earth will be blessed." This is a clear prophecy about the future Jewish Messiah and explains why both Matthew and Luke wrote extensive genealogies of Jesus in their Gospels. These genealogies demonstrate Jesus' connection to Abraham, and thus the prophecy in Genesis 12:3.

And consider this: If Satan were to somehow manage to destroy the Jewish race, he could conceivably short-circuit God's plan by preventing the Messiah from being born and bringing salvation to mankind. We see this sinister strategy in Pharaoh's attempt to kill all the Jewish male children in Exodus 1:16–2:20. However, the Genesis 12:3 prophecy kicked in (God's promise to curse those who cursed the Hebrews), and ultimately, the Jews were spared (Acts 7:18-19). Initially, Pharaoh's plan was thwarted by some honorable Hebrew midwives, and later by Moses himself, who led the Jews out of Egyptian slavery and ultimately to the Promised Land.

> Here is the irony: The devil has read the Bible. He knows how the story ends. And yet, blinded and self-deceived... he still somehow believes he can accomplish his goal.

We see Satan's hatred again through the Amalekites' determination to annihilate Israel and remove their presence from the land (Deuteronomy 25:17-19; Numbers 14:45; Judges 6:33; 1 Samuel 14:48). They too failed. Evil Haman attempted to have the Jews wiped out by persuading King Ahasuerus of Persia to turn against them. Had it not been for Queen Esther (a Jewess), he may well have succeeded. But fortunately, she was born "for such a time as this" (Esther 4:14).

King Herod ordered a massacre of the innocents in Matthew 2:16-17. Had he accomplished this task and murdered Mary's infant son, the child would not have grown up to fulfill His mission of providing salvation "to the Jew first and also to the Greek" (Romans 1:16-17). And if the Jewish leaders had understood "the wisdom" of God's prophecies concerning the Messiah, they never would've crucified the Lord (1 Corinthians 2:7-8).

All these examples illustrate that the evil perpetrated against the Jewish people by individuals and governments has an invisible, spiritual origin to it—one that is traceable back to Satan himself (see Ephesians 6:12).

You would think that with all the troubles, discriminatory hatred, false accusations, and unjust persecution the Jews have endured for thousands of years, Satan finally would have come to realize he can't win this battle. Given his many failures, you would think that by now, he would recognize that the legacy of the Jewish people cannot be erased.

You could think that. But you would be wrong.

Here is the irony: The devil has read the Bible. He knows how the story ends. And yet, blinded and self-deceived by his over-inflated pride, he still somehow believes he can accomplish his goal. He epitomizes the "belief in yourself" philosophy. And the following may shed some light on his rationalization. Satan remains in control of the kingdoms of this world, just as he did in Jesus' day. You will recall how the devil offered Christ rulership over all the kingdoms of the earth. And Jesus, in His response, did not dispute Satan's ability to do this (Matthew 4:8-9). It is these same territorial kingdoms that Satan will summon to Armageddon one day in a massive military effort to defeat and destroy the son of God and His heavenly armies (Revelation 16:12-16).

End-Times Animosity

Enter Revelation 12. There, John recorded the details about a pivotal moment that will occur at the midpoint of the seven-year tribulation. Following one last attempt to overthrow heaven's throne, Satan will be "thrown down" once again to Earth along with millions of his demonic disciples (verse 9). But this time, for good. This demoralizing defeat will ignite a fury in the devil not previously seen anywhere else in Scripture. He will explode with rage and wrath, "knowing that he has only a short time" (verse 12).

What happens next will cause the Holocaust itself to blush with evil envy.

I call it the Midpoint Massacre.

What we find in Revelation 12 are three coordinated attacks against the Jewish people, each of them displaying the devil's unbridled and unceasing animosity toward them.

Attack 1—Satan Persecutes Israel (Revelation 12:4; 13–14)

> When the dragon saw that he was thrown down to the earth, he persecuted the woman who gave birth to the male child (Revelation 12:13).

The Greek word John uses for "persecuted" is a word that means "to run swiftly after, aggressively chase, or hunt down." It is most often translated "persecute" in the New Testament.

Many commentators parallel Jesus' words in Matthew 24:9-10 to this passage. By this point in the tribulation, Antichrist has been mortally wounded and miraculously returned from the dead

(Revelation 13:3-4; 14). Immediately after this, he invades the Jewish Temple and the Holy of Holies. Inside that sacred room, he proclaims himself to the world as "God" (2 Thessalonians 2:3-4). This is the "abomination of desolation" Jesus spoke of in Matthew 24:15-16: "When you see the abomination of desolation which was spoken of through Daniel the prophet, standing in the holy place (let the reader understand), then those who are in Judea must flee to the mountains."

In other words, "RUN!"

This is the precise moment when the "*great* tribulation" officially begins (Matthew 24:21). Antichrist's persecution also coincides with the "mark of the beast" edict (Revelation 13:16-17). The choice could not be clearer at this time: worship Antichrist or die. And for the Jew, death is the only option as the man they once trusted turns out to be history's greatest blasphemer of their God. This is how viral and vitriolic Satan's hatred for Abraham's seed is.

In obedience to Christ's words in Matthew 24:16, the Jewish remnant will flee to the mountains, where she will find "a place prepared by God" (Revelation 12:6). God's provision for His people is made evident in verse 14: "The two wings of the great eagle were given to the woman, so that she could fly into the wilderness to her place, where she was nourished for a time and times and half a time, from the presence of the serpent."

Some Bible commentators believe this wilderness place may be in the area of Petra, in Bozrah. Micah 2:12 states,

> I will surely assemble all of you, Jacob,
> > I will surely gather the remnant of Israel.
> I will put them together like sheep in the *fold*;
> > Like a flock in the midst of its pasture
> > They will be noisy with men.

The Hebrew word translated "fold" is *bozrah* (meaning "sheep-fold"). Bozrah is in modern-day Jordan and is surrounded by protective cliffs and mountains. And, just like a sheepfold, it too has a narrow entrance (see Isaiah 33:16). Interestingly, the nation that will avoid being under Antichrist's control during the tribulation is modern-day Jordan (Daniel 11:41). The Lord will protect this godly remnant of Jews with the two wings of a great eagle, a likely reference to God Himself (Exodus 19:4; Deuteronomy 32:11; Isaiah 40:31). Unable to buy or sell because they have refused Antichrist's mark, God will supply these escapees with what they need, hiding them there in that wilderness refuge for three-and-a-half years (Revelation 12:6).

Attack 2—Satan Pours Out a River of Wrath Against Israel (Revelation 12:15-16)

> The serpent poured water like a river out of his mouth after the woman, so that he might cause her to be swept away with the flood (Revelation 12:15).

We do not know what this satanic flood will be, though John is likely using symbolic language here. But whatever strategy Antichrist employs with this river of wrath, it is conceivable this refers to some sort of military force (see Jeremiah 46:8; 47:2; Daniel 11:26; where the imagery of floods and water refer to military campaigns).

However, once again, the devil is prevented from reaching the Jews by the delivering power of God. Verse 14 states that the earth will help the woman: "The earth opened its mouth and drank up the river which the dragon poured out of his mouth." Perhaps in this case, the earth will literally open up and swallow Antichrist's attacking armies. That's similar to what happened to Pharaoh's army as the Egyptian soldiers went through the Red Sea (Exodus 14:21-28).

Attack 3—Satan Pursues All-Out War Against Israel (Revelation 12:17)

> The dragon was enraged with the woman, and went off to make war with the rest of her children, who keep the commandments of God and hold to the testimony of Jesus (Revelation 12:17).

After Satan's first two attacks have been thwarted by God, the dragon (Satan) and his false Christ (the beast) will become "enraged" with Israel. The devil's unrighteous anger knows no limits, and he will keep it laser-focused on God and His people. In verse 4, his hatred was directed at the Son at His birth. In verse 7, it is fixated on the Father in heaven. In verses 10-11, he channels his wrath toward tribulation-era Christians who have overcome his accusations and attacks because of "the blood of the Lamb and because of the word of their testimony," even if it means being martyred for Christ. Your future brethren would rather die a horrible death of beheading than deny their Lord by taking the Antichrist's mark (Revelation 13:7-10; 20:4).

In verses 6 and 13-16, we see Satan aggressively pursuing the Jews in an effort to wipe the memory of them from history. He will turn his attention toward "the rest" of Israel to "make war" with them. Though we are not told the precise identity of this group, there are a couple of possibilities here:

1. Tribulation Christians (Gentiles)—Those left behind or born during the tribulation who have trusted in Christ for salvation. The Bible describes Gentile believers as "Abraham's offspring" (Galatians 3:7, 29).

2. The 144,000 Jewish male evangelists (Revelation 7:3-8)— John makes special note that the dragon is enraged with "the

woman" (12:17), whom we know in context to be a reference to Israel (12:6, 13-15). So, it appears that "her children" must have a direct connection to the Jewish people. Though I cannot be dogmatic, it seems this group is also Jewish, and thus perhaps this is talking about the 144,000 or some other unknown believing Jewish remnant.

Global Hatred

What we do know is that somewhere in the course of Satan's or Antichrist's rampage, two-thirds of all the Jews alive at that time will be killed (Zechariah 13:8).

Prior to and simultaneous with these attacks, Jesus warned that Jewish believers would be delivered to persecution, killed, betrayed by other Jews, and turned over to Antichrist's authorities. He also prophesied that they would be "hated by *all nations* because of My name" (Matthew 24:9-10). Even family members will betray them (Mark 13:12; Luke 21:16). In short, the entire world will blame and persecute the Jews.

But what is Satan's rationale here? Though we don't have a chapter and verse that provides an answer, we can safely assume that if Satan can kill all the Jews, then they won't be around to cry out for a Savior to deliver them at His second coming. And if he can prevent Christ's return, Satan and his Antichrist can theoretically continue ruling the earth and be worshipped by mankind perpetually.

So where is all this hatred headed? And where will it culminate? From what we've seen in both history and Scripture's prophecies, we are presently ramping up to a time of global racial hatred against the Jewish people, a persecution building to a furious eruption during the tribulation. And how intense will this hatred be? Strong enough to kill on an unprecedented scale. Christians will also be swept up and persecuted in this end-times Holocaust (Revelation 6:9; 7:14; 13:7, 15).

Who will join in on this hatred? "All nations" (Matthew 24:9).

Where does this hatred come from? Satan himself, expressed through Antichrist and the false prophet. Like foot soldiers in a satanic army, billions will join this global hate party. In fact, so great will be the hate that when the two witnesses of Revelation 11 are finally killed by Antichrist, the whole earth will throw a massive party, with people giving gifts to one another in celebration of the deaths of God's Jewish prophets (verse 10). This reveals the depths of the hostility and animosity the world will have for the Jews and the prophecies concerning their Messiah.

How many Jews will die? Two-thirds of them, totaling likely into the millions (Zechariah 13:8).

Long ago, God promised the people of Israel that if they disobeyed Him, they would be dispersed to the nations, where they would "find no rest, and…no resting place for the soul of your foot" (Deuteronomy 28:65). And even after their regathering to the land (Isaiah 11:10-12) and being established as a nation again (Isaiah 66:7-8; Zechariah 12:3-6), they would still suffer through an unprecedented time of tribulation, during which the majority of them would perish (Zechariah 13:8-9).

However, God also promised to one day restore the people to Himself as they call upon Messiah at the close of the seven-year tribulation (Zechariah 12:10; 13:1). And thus, as Paul wrote, "all Israel will be saved" (Romans 11:25-29).

"Blame the Jews" is still Satan's battle cry. It's still his maniacal marketing strategy. To date, he has thrown everything (including the kitchen sink) at the Jewish people. And yet here they are. Still alive. Still thriving. And now, living once again in the land promised to them (Genesis 12:7; 13:15-17; 15:18-21). Make no mistake about it: According to the Bible, that land belongs to God, and it is His prerogative to give it to whomever He pleases (Leviticus 25:23; Psalm 115:3). Though the devil and the nations try to annihilate the Jewish people, they will last as long as the "fixed order of the heavens" (Jeremiah 31:35-37).

The seismic event of Adam's fall into sin has had a ripple effect that continues to this day, with devastating viruses, godlessness, lawlessness, anarchy, and a renewed goal for a globalist agenda. And like the ancient Roman roads that made it much easier for people to reach their destinations, the devil is paving the way for his Antichrist to make his debut. He is already beginning his final push to exterminate Israel and every trace of the Jewish people. A new strain of Jewish hatred is emerging, one that blames them for global viruses, economic downturns, and even racial unrest and injustice.

And it doesn't end there, as Scripture tells us a second Holocaust is on the horizon.

Following a three-and-a-half-year deceptive ruse, the bloodiest chapter in Israel's history will be unleashed upon them and on display for all the world to see. But until that time, Satan will continue leveraging aftershocks from recent world calamities to serve his agenda and shift the universal narrative toward an anti-Israel, antisemitic spirit.

Meanwhile, for us as Christians, we have a threefold mandate as it relates to Israel: first, to pray for the peace of Jerusalem (Psalm 122:6). Ultimately, this prayer will be answered in the millennial kingdom, when Jesus reigns from Jerusalem, and therefore is synonymous with praying, "Your kingdom come. Your will be done, on earth as it is in heaven" (Matthew 6:10). Second, to bless Israel (Genesis 12:3), supporting her survival and defense against her encircling enemies, and third, to make disciples of Jesus from among the Jewish people (Matthew 28:18-20). Individual Jews are not guaranteed forgiveness and heaven, but only those who call upon Jesus as their Messiah (Acts 4:11-12). Like the rest of the world, Jews need Jesus too.

Chapter 7

TIMES OF THE SIGNS

Signs.

They're everywhere. Signs advertising businesses and restaurants. Signs that communicate important information or are used to market everything from legal services to junk food. Some signs give direction while others warn of danger. There are caution signs, safety signs, construction signs, and signs identifying where you are. Signs come in many shapes, sizes, and colors. Big. Small. Green. Yellow. Square. Rectangular. Circular. Octagonal. Most all signs serve a discernable purpose, even if that purpose is just to make you notice it's there.

Signs are especially prevalent on roadways. They can appear atop a roadside post, on a billboard, or perched above the highway. They can even be painted on the road itself.

They can let you know you're going the right direction or confirm that you're lost. Signs can prompt you to turn around or alter your route. They tell you how far away you are from your destination, how far you've drifted from it, or reveal exactly where you are on a map. Signs are especially helpful when you're approaching the endpoint of your journey.

Some signs are too far off in the distance to clearly discern and read, while others sneak up on you, and before you know it, you've already passed them. Other signs are old, outdated, faded, irrelevant, or even misleading.

At times, signs contain so much information they're difficult to read as you pass them on the road. I suppose that's why most people today allow their smartphone's AI voice to guide them. Relying on GPS can be much easier and safer than trying to figure out directions for yourself.

Finally, it's important to know which signs to look for—which ones apply to you, and which ones are okay to ignore.

Sign Language

The Bible has a lot to say about signs, particularly those that point to the prophetic last days. In the Old Testament, two separate words are used 116 times to describe promised signs and wonders to and for Israel. In the New Testament, the Greek word translated "sign" is *semeion* and is used nearly 80 times, referring in almost every instance to something (usually miraculous in nature) that confirms or corroborates God's Word. This word describes everything from the miracles of Jesus to those performed by demons in Revelation.

Since the close of the New Testament canon, we have not been living in an age of overt signs and wonders. Though God can and does still perform miracles, since the first century, His primary method for convincing people of the truth has been His Spirit working through the Word of God (Luke 16:27-31; John 16:8-11). However, during the tribulation, the world will once again experience an age of supernatural signs and wonders. In fact, they will be commonplace, originating both from God and His prophets as well as from Satan, his demons, and false prophets (Matthew 24:11, 24; 2 Thessalonians 2:9-12; Revelation 11:3-14; 13:13-14; 16:13-14).

But when it comes to the signs of the end times, there can be a lot of confusion. That's because one of the problems with signs (both the highway variety and the biblical kind) is that they can be misread, misinterpreted, and even missed altogether. Some signs are even covered up or hidden because it's not time yet for them to be revealed.

There is a subculture of Christians and prophecy enthusiasts today who are quasi-fanatical about watching for and even seeking out prophetic signs. This leads many to misidentify or mislabel an occurrence as a biblical sign when, in fact, it is not.

How can we be certain that a sign really is a sign? How can we know whether what we perceive as a prophetic harbinger is merely someone's personal belief, perspective, or opinion? Or whether it's nothing at all?

What is the difference between a cultural, global, religious, or moral *trend* and a genuine biblical sign that points to a prophetic event? And how can we know when the two are one and the same? Further, how can we develop the discernment to know that difference?

Fortunately, when we attempt to decipher biblical signs, there are seven solid principles to guide us and help us avoid potholes and traps along the way.

Principle 1—Current phenomenon (natural disasters, pandemics, cosmic events, etc.) are not specific fulfillments of end-times Bible prophecy.

They do, however, demonstrate that such catastrophic events (as predicted in Revelation) *do* occur, thus lending credibility to

Scripture. They also serve to direct our eyes toward the prophetic future, during which similar events will actually occur.

Principle 2—Some prophecies contain missing pieces of information, supplying us with only part of a much larger puzzle.

For example, Micah 5:2 tells us the Messiah would be born in Bethlehem. But it tells us nothing of His mission or the exact nature of His birth. For example, we have to consult Isaiah 7:14 to discover that He would be born of a virgin. There are many individual prophecies that serve as clues pointing to a greater mystery not yet revealed. With limited information in hand, we are often tempted to try to solve the entire puzzle prematurely. That's why it's important to read the whole Bible and get the big picture. Doing so helps us see how each piece fits into God's overall prophetic narrative.

Principle 3—Some supposed signs may *look* like prophecy in the making, but in time prove to be something different, or even unrelated to Scripture altogether.

To an untrained eye, the fertilized egg of a starfish is indistinguishable from that of a human. And the developing fetus of a chimpanzee is almost identical to a human baby in the womb. Therefore, at first glance, an inexperienced onlooker might arrive at a faulty conclusion regarding which species he or she is looking at. The same is true with what people sometimes perceive to be signs but aren't. I call this the mistaken identity principle.

Principle 4—Some prophecies are in process.

There are what we could call sub-signs or sneak previews that point to actual biblical signs and prophecies. When you see a new house being built but only the foundation and framework are visible, you can still be relatively sure the finished product will look like a house (rather than an office building or a barn). Similarly, prophecies in their embryonic or developmental stage help us envision what's coming, though not necessarily with absolute clarity. For example, today's technology would make it easy to implement the mark of the beast (see chapter 4), yet we still do not know exactly what form the mark will take. We could call these foreshocks, previews, harbingers, or precursors leading to the actual prophetic birth pangs Jesus spoke of in Matthew 24:8. But they are not the signs themselves.

Principle 5—Some prophecies are on the horizon.

This is complementary to the principle above. In this case, we may see what look like prophecies forming in the distance, but the *timing* of their fulfillment cannot be known. Several times, my wife and I made the long trip across the vast state of Texas to visit my then-Army son and his family at Fort Bliss in El Paso. At some point on this seemingly endless 15-hour journey, we would reach a spot where we could finally see the Franklin Mountains range of El Paso in the distance. This sight gave us hope, letting us know we were nearing the end of our journey. However, there was one small problem. The West Texas desert can be cruelly deceptive, tricking one's eyes and distorting the distance that remains between you and your destination. I would say to my wife, "Don't get too excited. We're not there *yet*." What appeared to be the final hour of our drive ended up taking much, much longer.

This can happen with Bible prophecy too. Just because we may be getting a glimpse of distant end-times prophecies doesn't necessarily mean they are about to be fulfilled in the immediate future. They *could* be, but not necessarily.

Principle 6—Some signs are not prophetic at all, but rather manufactured sensationalism.

Blood moons. Planetary alignments. Jewish feasts. Catastrophic weather events. Even supposed alien spacecraft sightings. All of these have been cited by enthusiastic prophecy promoters as harbingers of the last days. Case in point: It was claimed by some "experts" that on September 23, 2017, Revelation 12:1-2 would be fulfilled in the heavens before our very eyes, signifying the rapture would occur. This prophetic propaganda narrative stated that the sun would be in the constellation Virgo—"a woman clothed with the sun," and that "the moon under her feet" referred to the nine stars of the constellation Leo (plus Mercury, Venus, and Mars,) totaling "twelve stars" at Virgo's head. Soon after this, Jupiter would be positioned at her center—corresponding to "she was with child."

They claimed that after September 23, Jupiter would travel east, past Virgo's feet—that is, "she cried out, being in labor and in pain to give birth." And because Jupiter is the largest planet in our solar system, it is the "king"—or "she gave birth to a son, a male child, destined to rule all the nations with an iron rod" (verse 5).

Confused yet?

All these phenomena were a convincing sign to some prophecy aficionados that the rapture was about to occur. Never mind that this same planetary alignment had occurred at least four times in the last thousand years (1056, 1293, 1483, 1827). Of course, to a biblically untrained mind, this might seem like a perfectly reasonable interpretation of Revelation 12:1-2. After all, the planets, stars, sun, and moon are real, and they're put in the sky for us to observe, just like the Bible says (Psalm 19:1). Plus, didn't Joel and Peter both state that in the last days there would be "wonders in the sky" (Joel 2:30; Acts 2:19)? So what's to doubt? It's real, right? A bona fide last-days prophetic fulfillment...or not?

Aside from the fact that these phenomena have occurred four previous times, the deeper problem here is that Revelation 12:1-2 has nothing whatsoever to do with stars and constellations. Rather, they represent Israel, her 12 tribes, and the Messiah's birth, as the subsequent verses in that passage clearly explain.

Nevertheless, thousands were convinced this interpretation was correct—so much so that a film crew from Los Angeles flew out to my home to interview me for a DirecTV documentary called "The Sign." I was joined by others—rabbis, authors, and prophecy experts from around the world—to discuss these wonders. As it turned out, I was the lone voice arguing for a scripturally based interpretation of Revelation 12:1-2.

Knowing how to properly interpret Scripture will save you from falling for such speculative nonsense.

Other proposed end-time signs include blood moons, which are more directly mentioned in prophecy, and are, in fact, apocalyptic (Joel 2:31; Acts 2:20; Revelation 6:12). However, these are *not* a specific fulfillment of Bible prophecy. Blood moons (lunar eclipses) can and do appear, but past occurrences prove only that fact. Regardless of how close such a phenomenon may be to a Jewish holiday or feast, they do not automatically or authoritatively signify the arrival of prophetic fulfillment. Plus, the fact that nothing biblically prophetic has yet to happen in conjunction with these lunar eclipses proves the point.

If anything, these past occurrences are a case of misunderstanding prophecy, misinterpreting Scripture, and misapplying it to our lives (see Principle 3). Besides, the prophetic blood moon we see in Revelation 6:12 will be unique, supernatural, and much more severe than any previous phenomenon. It will also be accompanied by meteor showers and massive tectonic-altering earthquakes (verses 13-14). This is why we must be cautious about viewing heavenly events as being prophetic in nature.

This principle also applies to what many call newspaper exegesis, where seemingly every Middle Eastern or geopolitical headline is somehow made to correlate to Bible prophecy. This is *not* to say that some current events are unrelated to the stage-setting aspect of prophecy. But again, great caution must be taken, especially in these last days, not to sound the trumpet of prophetic alarm every time a rocket is hurled at Israel or some rogue world leader acts in an Antichrist-like manner.

Principle 7—Caution about personal revelations.

Hardly a week goes by without a pastor, internet preacher, or prophetic pundit claiming he or she has received information about the end times via an audible prophecy, vision, dream, or through studying numerology or Jewish calendars. There are several reasons we can't and shouldn't trust such claims.

First, they are 100 percent *un*verifiable. In other words, how is anyone to know with any degree of certainty that this direct revelation is, in fact, *from God*? A "thus saith the Lord" statement is a very serious assertion and should be carefully examined against what Scripture says. And are there ever authenticating miracles and supernatural wonders accompanying such claims? Never. So essentially they are unprovable, and thus are unreliable.

Second, they are typically vague in nature. For example, someone will say, "A great revival will sweep the nation this year…" These so-called prophecies end up being more like nebulous horoscopes or fortune cookie slips than divine revelations from God. And in time, they too prove to be false.

Third, individual prophetic revelations ceased when the last apostle died. According to Ephesians 2:20, the apostles and prophets of long ago have already built and completed Christianity's foundation, and Jude 3 speaks of "the faith which was *once and for all* handed down to the saints." Therefore, I do not believe new or ongoing special revelations are still being given to the church. Rather, God wants His people to know and study the extensive revelation He has *already* given to her in the Bible.

Sadly, many Christians today are quick to ignore Scripture while confidently trusting in their own experiences and emotions. If their claims of modern-day supernatural communication truly are from God, they would be binding upon the whole body of Christ. But direct revelation was given to the apostles and prophets alone, and the New Testament writers completed the authoritative "truth foundation" of the church during the New Testament era. When the ink dried on Revelation 22:21, special divine revelation ceased.

Further, God makes it clear that His Word is all we need, especially as it relates to doctrine and end-times prophecy (2 Timothy 3:16-17; 2 Peter 1:3). This point is made emphatically in the final passage in Revelation:

> I testify to everyone who hears the words of this prophecy of this book: if anyone *adds* to them, God shall add to him the plagues which are written in this book; and if anyone *takes away* from the words of the book of this prophecy, God will take away his part from the tree of life and from the holy city, which are written in this book (Revelation 22:18-19).

I can't imagine the Lord being any more specific than that. His is a stern and potentially damnable warning to anyone who professes to speak authoritatively for Him with new truth not already revealed in Scripture. The penalty for such prophetic claims puts these "last-days prophets" in eternal danger. Their proclamations are an insult to the Word of God and to God Himself. Their actions portray the depth of their self-deception as well as the height of their arrogance.

These self-appointed proponents of new revelations are not treating God's completed revelation, the Bible, with the utmost reverence and respect. As a result, they will find themselves on the receiving end of the divine warning in Revelation 22:18-19—which comes *from God*. Add to His book and you'll likely find yourself left behind to endure the plagues and judgments of Revelation. So don't try to make prophecy say what it is not saying, and don't make your own words out to be God's words.

A second warning in Revelation 22:19 is aimed at "anyone [who] takes away from the words of the book of this prophecy."[1] This would apply to any who attempt to explain away Revelation by weakening, trivializing, or dismissing its prophecies. Every single prophecy concerning Jesus' first coming was amazingly specific and was fulfilled literally. Apart from some symbolic speech in Revelation (much of which John himself explains for us), the future prophecies given in Revelation will also be fulfilled literally and exactly as written. Those believers who deliberately edit or delete the prophecies in this book risk losing their eternal reward (verse 19). Though one's view of the end times is not a salvation issue, it is entirely possible that those who deliberately dismiss or explain away Revelation's contents may have never known Christ to begin with (Matthew 7:21-23).

To summarize, we should not alter, add to, or tamper with the established biblical text—*ever* (Deuteronomy 4:2; 12:32; Proverbs 30:6; Jeremiah 26:2; Revelation 1:3).

Biblical Billboards

Now that we've set aside false signs and fabricated visions, are there any *actual* signs of the times out there telling us the rapture and Revelation could be nearer than we think? That is a perfectly reasonable question, and Jesus' disciples asked that very thing a few days before His crucifixion. While on the Mount of Olives they asked Him, "Tell us, when will these things happen, and what will be the sign of Your coming, and of the end of the age?" (Matthew 24:3).

Jesus responded by launching into a discourse on Bible prophecy, the first part of which (Matthew 24:4-14) directly parallels Revelation 6–7. But before He revealed anything, He issued a critical warning: "See to it that no one misleads you. For many will come in my name, saying, 'I am the Christ,' and will mislead many" (Matthew 24:4-5).

Throughout history there have been false messiahs, and there are even some today. One is a man who goes by the name Vissarion, also known as the "Christ of Siberia." This man is a former traffic officer turned Russian mystic who founded the Church of the Last Testament in a remote Siberian village. Allegedly, he received a revelation from God at the time the Soviet Union collapsed and was told that he was Jesus Christ "reborn." How convenient. His cult has now swelled to more than 5,000 followers, many of whom live with him in his village commune.[2]

For reasons we will see in the next chapter, more false messiahs will emerge in the end of days.

But getting back to our question: What are some actual last-days prophecies that have either been fulfilled or are in the stage-setting era?

Sign 1—The Jews Return to the Holy Land

This is considered by many to be the most-prophesied event of the end times (Jeremiah 30:1-51; Ezekiel 34:11-24; 37:1-28; Zechariah 10:6-10). In fact, the Jewish nation must be reborn and living in their ancient homeland to make the events of Revelation possible. Virtually everything that occurs in the end times hinges on the existence of Israel as a nation, including the peace covenant that officially inaugurates the seven-year tribulation (Daniel 9:27), the pivotal midpoint abomination of desolation (Daniel 9:27; Matthew 24:15; Thessalonians 2:4), and "all Israel" becoming saved at the close of the tribulation (Romans 11:25-26; Hosea 6:1-3; Zechariah 12:10). This return to the land was and is a process that began with the Zionist movement of the late 1800s. However, following their establishment as a nation on May 14, 1948, Jewish people have continued to pour into Israel from all over the world.

The Jews are the only ethnic or people group in history to retain their identity after having been scattered to more than 70 countries for more than 2,000 years. Today, more Jews are living in the land than at any time since AD 70, with some 6.8 million currently there.[3] So many Jews are flooding into Israel from around the world that the Israeli government is concerned it won't be able to contain them all.[4]

How can we explain this historically unprecedented phenomenon? Simple. The Jews are being called home by God, just like He said He would do. The existence of Israel, then, is *the* miracle of the twentieth century, opening the floodgates and making it possible for the prophecies in Revelation to be fulfilled. This is why the rebirth of Israel is called the super sign of end-times prophecy.

Sign 2—Globalism and a One-World Government

As we learned back in chapter 2, we are currently in the midst of a shift toward a globalist, centralized government. Ultimately, this will result in the rebirth (or final form) of the ancient Roman Empire (Daniel 2:41-44; 7:7-8, 24; 11:36-38; Revelation 6:2; 13:2; 17:10-12). This formation likely will be facilitated by weakening nations who are in need of viability and a supported economic infrastructure following a future global black-swan event. The Bible states this new world order of government will exist in a ten-nation alliance headed by "the beast" (Revelation 13:1-2). Some aspect, reformation, or restructuring of the current European Union *may* contribute toward forming this coming kingdom. Or it could be a coalition somewhat unrelated to previous or present-day international alliances.

This global government is an essential element of Satan's strategy of establishing his Antichrist as world ruler. All that is needed is a big-enough international crisis that justifies the formation of such a coalition. In the meantime, the world will continue pursuing unity—technologically, economically, and geopolitically. Nationalism and patriotism are being frowned upon and even demonized in some cultures, with a "global citizen" spirit gaining momentum in their place.[5] Undeniably, as more nations experience economic calamity, we will continue moving toward an alliance-based, centralized global governing body. And the devil will have a man waiting in the wings, standing at the ready to take the reins and unite planet Earth.

Sign 3—The Push for Peace in the Middle East

Scripture tells us that in the last days, a major peace treaty will be established between the Antichrist and Israel (Danial 9:27; 1 Thessalonians 5:1-3; Revelation 6:1-2). The ongoing tensions and conflicts between Israel and the surrounding Muslim nations threaten the peace of the entire planet and could easily catapult us into World War III. Every US president in modern history has proposed plans for peace and compromise. In 2017, it was suggested that Israel and Palestine officially join the European Union in order to settle some of their disputes. Both declined to do so. More recently, President

Donald Trump's "Deal of the Century" was offered as a partial solution to this political powder keg. It too failed to achieve its objective, though subsequent efforts enabled him to successfully broker the Abraham Accords Peace Agreement, which Israeli prime minister Benjamin Netanyahu called the "dawn of a new Middle East."[6] Among its provisions is opening up travel between the UAE, Bahrain, and Israel and allowing citizens of those Arab countries to visit holy sites in Israel, including the Al-Aqsa Mosque on the Temple Mount in Jerusalem. Netanyahu also proclaimed that this peace "will eventually expand to other Arab states, and ultimately end the Arab-Israeli conflict once and for all."[7]

However, this is *not* the peace covenant spoken of in Daniel 9:27 (though Antichrist could indeed build upon such peace agreements).

But the fact remains that peace in the Middle East is among the world's top geopolitical priorities, and that it *is* prophesied to occur. And when it does, it will officially mark the beginning of the seven-year tribulation. Present-day peace accords, then, are stage-setting signs that point to a future time when the entire world is in labor pains.

Sign 4—Jewish Temple Rebuilt

In order for Antichrist to commit the abomination of desolation prophesied by Daniel, Jesus, and Paul, the Jewish Temple *must* be rebuilt on the Temple Mount in Jerusalem (Daniel 9:27; 11:31; Matthew 24:15; 2 Thessalonians 2:3-4; Revelation 13:14-15). Keep in mind there hasn't been a temple in Jerusalem since AD 70, when the Roman general Titus invaded that city and destroyed the Hebrew house of worship (just as Jesus prophesied in Matthew 24:2 and Luke 19:43-44). Most likely the peace treaty that Antichrist brokers will help facilitate the construction of this Temple at the beginning of the tribulation.

Scripture confirms with a 100-percent degree of certainty that a third Temple will be built. And a lot has already happened to prepare the way for its construction.

In 1987, the Temple Institute was founded in Jerusalem in anticipation of a future rebuilt Temple.[8] They have already drawn up detailed blueprints, fashioned sacred Temple vessels and utensils, constructed altars, and sewn priestly garments according to Old Testament specifications. They regularly hold training courses for aspiring priests, having trained more than 500 to date who are descendants of the tribe of Levi. They have offered sacrifices just outside the Temple Mount, once again in anticipation of the day when they will do the same inside the rebuilt Temple.

In June 2020, the Institute announced the continued close inspection of two red heifers, the first to be born in 2,000 years. Jewish religious leaders believe the birth of a red heifer will precede the construction of the third Temple. They assert that only the red heifer "can restore the biblical purity needed to rebuild the temple."[9]

This contingency of Jews is ready, waiting for the peace plan that will enable them to secure the place needed on the Temple Mount to begin construction. And at no time in the past 2,000 years has this been even remotely possible.

That is, until *now*.

Sign 5—A Growing Apostasy

The Bible prophesies that in the last days there will be a great falling away or departure from God's truth (1 Timothy 4:1-3; 2 Timothy 3:1-9, 13; 2 Thessalonians 2:3; Jude 1-16). This departure will be marked by open compromise, including both subtle and overt attacks on Scripture. It will also involve distorting, doubting, and even denying the clear teachings of God's Word. In recent years, we've seen a renewed assault on the inerrancy of

Scripture, the denial and reinterpretation of the Genesis creation account, and the dismissal of the Bible's authority with regard to basic morality. One well-known former megachurch preacher openly denigrated God's Word by stating that the church cannot remain relevant to the culture if it "quotes letters from 2000 years ago as their best defense."[10]

> The things taking place in our world not only foreshadow the Revelation generation but also mirror the days of Noah.

Paul wrote, "The Spirit explicitly says that in later times some will fall away from the faith, paying attention to deceitful spirits and doctrines of demons" (1 Timothy 4:1). A direct result of denying God His rightful place of preeminence, an entire generation is currently plunging itself into a new Dark Ages. Blinded by their sin-hardened hearts, they foolishly speculate regarding truth, life, humanity, sexuality, marriage, and even God (Romans 1:21; 1 Corinthians 2:14; Ephesians 4:17). This naturally results in a society immersed in idolatry, sexual immorality, homosexuality, violence, slander, hatred of God, destruction of the family, unreasonable and unsupportable belief systems, unloving relationships, unforgiving hearts, and the unashamed public celebration of all manner of deviant sin (Romans 1:24-32; 2 Timothy 3:1-5, 13).

This ever-expanding trend will see its ultimate fulfillment during the tribulation through Antichrist's false religion (Revelation 17:1-18) and is also part of what will bring the judgments of Revelation 6–19 upon them (2 Thessalonians 2:10-12; Revelation 9:20-21; 16:6, 9, 11, 21).

The things taking place in our world not only foreshadow the Revelation generation, but also mirror the days of Noah. Jesus said in Matthew 24:36 that the time of His coming would "be just like the days of Noah." We live in a sin-soaked and unrepentant culture that rejects God and all things good, while actively pursuing and defending evil and wickedness. This apostasy is a neon flashing sign that indicates the days of the tribulation may not be far away. Though a last-days revival is not prophesied in Scripture, a last-days apostasy *is*.

Sign 6—The Mark of the Beast (Revelation 13:16-17)

I have already addressed the nature and viability of the "*mark* of the beast" (Greek, *charagma*) in chapter 4. And by way of reminder, technologically speaking, such a mark is possible right now. So this is no longer a question of technology but of practicality and prescription. In other words, when will there be a mandate or a need for it?

When the controversial COVID masks were dictated by various national, state, and local municipalities in the name of public health, people across the world begin feeling the effects of not only global uniformity, but also the squeeze of governmental authority on their necks. And though some states and countries were less restrictive than others, there will be no such leniency when the Antichrist and his fellow beast, the false prophet, rise to power. Refusal of service, fines, and even arrest will be off the table this time, as the penalty for not bearing his mark will be death. No reprieve. No appeal. And no mercy. Put plainly: Refuse to get the mark and worship Antichrist as God Almighty, and you *will* be killed (Revelation 13:15; 20:4).

All that is left now is for this coming world leader to rise out of the sea of humanity and step onto the shores of history. And that is another guaranteed sign (Daniel 9:26-27; 11:36-45; Matthew 24:21-24; 2 Thessalonians 2:3-9; 1 John 2:18, 22; 2 John 7; Revelation 6:1-2; 13:1-18).

Sign 7—Increasing Persecution

We explored in chapter 6 the history and prophecy regarding the Jewish people and the next horrific Holocaust. And during that time of tribulation, there will also be a global effort to massacre Christians (Revelation 6:9-11; 13:7-10, 15; 20:4). Following the rapture, many who are left behind will repent, crying out to Jesus for salvation. I believe this will occur as a result of several key influences:

1. The mass disappearance of believers will get their attention, bringing them to their knees to trust Christ.

2. Others will "divinely stumble" upon a book, podcast, recording, testimony, video, or Bible.

3. Some will observe what's happening in the world, along with the appearance of Antichrist, and, prompted by the Holy Spirit, put two and two together, becoming convinced of the gospel and Bible prophecy, which they had heard at some point in the past.

4. They will hear the preaching of the two witnesses (Revelation 11:1-10) or the 144,000 Jewish male evangelists (Revelation 7:4-8).

5. They will hear the angel who flies around the globe calling sinners to "fear God and give him glory…and worship him" (Revelation 14:6).

But even though a great multitude will be saved during this time, the vast majority of people will not. Most will be deceived into believing Antichrist through his deceptive wonders and through a spirit of delusion sent by God Himself (2 Thessalonians 2:10-12). These tribulation-era Christians will suffer at the hands of Antichrist, and perhaps also from the rest of humanity as well. Devoid of the sin-restraining influence of the Holy Spirit, people will be filled with evil along with a hatred for God and all those who follow Jesus Christ. They will turn on these new believers with a mob-like fury, turning in or killing every Christian they can find (John 15:18-22; Revelation 6:9-11).

But Satan is not content to wait until the tribulation to go after Jesus' followers. Presently, Christians are being actively persecuted in 150 countries, affecting an estimated 250 million believers.[11] Every month, an average of 105 churches are attacked, burned, or vandalized. Eleven of our brethren are martyred every day for their faith.[12] There are forced church closings. Bible burnings. Pastors being arrested. And that's just here in the USA right now![13]

Growing persecution from government, anarchist organizations, and a non-Christian pagan culture and media are all indications that the heat is being turned up on Jesus' bride. Satan simply does not want us to meet, worship, or function as the church.[14] In other countries, believers are beaten, attacked, tormented, and killed for their faith in Christ. Their homes are set on fire, their daughters raped and dismembered, and their pastors tortured or sent to prison. Rest assured, Satan will continue strategizing ways to persecute Jesus' body and bride leading up to the final apocalyptic mass murder of Christians in the tribulation.

Sign 8—The Mount of Olives

How does a mountain qualify as a sign of the end times? Well, it's not the mountain itself, but the prophecy concerning that mountain that is so compelling (Zechariah 14:4; Acts 1:11; Matthew 24:3). In the Zechariah passage, it says this about Jesus' return to Earth at His second coming: "On that day His feet will stand on the Mount of Olives, which is in front of Jerusalem on the east; and the Mount of Olives will be split in its middle from east to west forming a very large valley. Half of the mountain will move toward the north, and the other half toward the south."

The touchdown location for Jesus' descent from heaven could be on the exact spot from where He ascended in Acts 1:9-10. And when His feet hit dirt, there will be an earthquake that will split the Mount of Olives in half. But in what way is this a sign pointing toward the end times when this event won't occur until the very *end* of the seven-year tribulation? Just this: In 2004, a three-year study by the Geological Survey of Israel discovered this same Mount of Olives to be at *imminent* risk for an earthquake. And what's even more amazing is that they detected the fault line running right through the middle of the mountain runs *east to west*![15] This fits perfectly with what Zechariah prophesied 2,500 years ago.

Of course, God doesn't need an existing fault line in place for Jesus to split the mountain in half. I suspect He allowed this discovery for the purpose of building our faith and giving the world even more evidence of the trustworthiness of His Word and the credibility of Bible prophecy. Yes, the Mount of Olives is both a sign *and* a wonder, just waiting for the right Person to trigger the prophetic promise that it will one day be split.

What Are the Odds?

Now, it is possible, though not intellectually honorable, to look at the eight above-mentioned signs and previews and to conclude they are all simply coincidences. Accidental happenings. Nothing more than just a collective fluke of chance. You could say the Bible just got lucky, as in *really* lucky. So lucky that every single prophecy is obviously in formation.

Or you could look at the evidence and conclude that God's

prophecies have a 100 percent probability of coming true. If that's your conclusion, then you're on the right side of prophetic history.

Thousands of years ago, God's Word predicted certain events and phenomena would take place during humanity's final days. And the evidence strongly suggests that they have either seen their ful-fillment—as with the rebirth of Israel—or are in the developmen-tal stages of being realized.

It was Jesus who said that these very signs, and more, would "merely [be] the beginning of birth pangs" (Matthew 24:8). By definition, genuine birth pangs (labor pains) do not occur at the moment of conception or at any other time during the pregnancy. Rather, they occur right before the actual birth.

From what we see taking place around us today, we can reason-ably say that our present world is *pregnant* with prophetic previews. And it's only a matter of time before these end-times contractions grow stronger and increase in frequency. Just like actual birth pains.

Yes, we're living in the times of the signs.

Chapter 8

THE COMING SUPER CRISIS

On a spring morning in 1918, a US Army cook named Albert Gitchell, then stationed in Kansas, went to the hospital with a 104-degree fever. Within a month, some 1,000 of his fellow soldiers were also hospitalized. And because some of these troops were deployed overseas, the illness spread like wildfire, invading French and British ranks and eventually infecting 50 to 75 percent of their soldiers.

When fall rolled around, a new strain of the virus had developed. So deadly was this second wave that a healthy person could show symptoms in the morning and be dead by the same evening. As troops moved around the world and then back home, the pandemic spread to general populations, killing young and old alike. In January 1919, a third wave arose in Australia, killing thousands more. All told, in just two years, more than 500 million people were infected, representing about two-thirds of Earth's population. Though estimates vary, somewhere between 17 to 50 million people eventually perished because of Gitchell's pandemic, now known as the Spanish Flu.[1]

Within two decades, the world would suffer even more crippling crises. The stock market crash of 1929. Germany's invasion of Poland in September 1939, which thrust Europe into World War II. Soon afterward, the United States was attacked at Pearl Harbor by Japan, forcing our country into that global conflict.

Though peace was eventually achieved in 1945, this would by no means be the end of war or of the threat of it. The Korean conflict emerged in the early 1950s. This was followed by the Cuban missile crisis in October 1962, which had millions across the world holding their breath as Russia and the United States stared down one another to see who would blink. One kneejerk response would have likely catapulted Western civilization into a nuclear holocaust. Then came November 22, 1963, and the assassination of a US president in broad daylight.

On September 11, 2001, America's way of life once again suddenly came to a screeching halt, sending us to our knees, and once more, into battle. Since that time, it seems there has been an endless chain reaction of catastrophes across the world: mass shootings, suicide bombings, terrorist attacks, pandemics and plagues, tsunamis, hurricanes, massive earthquakes, floods, heat waves, famines, volcanic eruptions, tropical cyclones, and other calamities that have snuffed out the lives of millions.

Crises.

"Behold, I Tell You a Mystery"

We've looked at the impact of 2020, with the coronavirus pandemic and its ripple-effect aftershocks. These have had cumulative effect and worn the world emotionally thin, leaving everyone wondering what disastrous plight awaits us next. We cringe whenever we hear or see the words *Breaking News*. It feels as though there is a universal dread hovering over us like foreboding storm clouds. We wonder what new black-swan event lurks around the corner. It begs the question, "What's next?" What event looms on the horizon, poised to once again redefine our existence and change the course of human history?

Fortunately for Christians, the answer has already been recorded within the pages of the Bible. It is a 2,000-year-old prophecy, given during an age of great crisis and persecution for the early church. It is a sign-less event, meaning there are no foreshocks that will announce its arrival. Unlike other future prophecies that may currently be in their developmental stages, thus giving us clues concerning their formation, the same cannot be said about this one. No precursors or pre-signs *must* take place for this prophecy to occur. There will be no immediate warnings. No blaring alarms. And no potential calendar dates to circle ahead of time marking its coming fulfillment. Instead, it is portrayed in Scripture as imminent, meaning it can take place at any time, at any moment.

Search the Bible all you want, but you will not find a single verse that reveals the precise timing of this coming event. We are not told *when* it will happen, only *that* it will occur. It is like the unannounced arrival of a king or a surprise visit by a dignitary. Or as Scripture portrays it, like a bridegroom's sudden appearance to snatch away his beloved betrothed.

In Scripture, this event is known by many names—the appearing (Titus 2:13), the coming (Hebrews 10:37; Revelation 22:7, 12, 20), our salvation (1 Thessalonians 5:9), the revelation (1 Corinthians 1:7), the gathering together (2 Thessalonians 2:1), and the blessed hope (Titus 2:13).

But you know it by its most popular designation: the rapture.

What exactly is this rapture? Why doesn't everyone believe it will take place? And if it is real, then are there any clues at all that indicate when it could occur, generally speaking? And when it does, how will it change us and affect the world?

What Is the Rapture?

The word *rapture* refers to the moment in time when Jesus Christ will return in the sky to snatch away His bride and take her to heaven. According to the pre-tribulational rapture view, in doing so, His bride will be delivered from God's coming wrath *prior* to the tribulation (Revelation 6–19). Others see the rapture as taking place at the *midpoint* of that seven-year period (the mid-trib view), about *three-fourths* of the way into the tribulation (the pre-wrath view), or at the *very end* of the tribulation (the post-trib view). All of these views, with the exception of the pre-tribulation view, have the church enduring the judgments of Revelation (though adherents of the mid-trib view claim the judgments that occur during the first half of the tribulation are a result of *man's* wrath, not God's).

Not every Christian or theologian believes in the rapture. One of the objections to the idea of the rapture is that the word itself is not found in Scripture, and therefore it is a *nonexistent* doctrine. And it is true that the word itself is not found in any English translation of the Bible, for the same reasons we don't find other words like *Easter*, *Christmas*, *incarnation*, *missions*, *Great Commission*, and *Trinity*—or *Bible*, for that matter. That's because these are all English words coined by people to describe teachings and doctrines that *are* found in the Bible. They are names and designations that help us to better understand Scripture in our own language. More important than what we call a certain doctrine is whether it is actually taught in Scripture.

Some go so far as to dismiss the teaching of the rapture as a dangerous doctrine. British Theologian N.T. Wright called it "a pseudo-theological version of home alone" that has "reportedly frightened many children into some kind of (distorted) faith."[2] Others claim the concept of the rapture is a recent doctrine, not a historic and biblical one. They allege the origins of the doctrine of the rapture can be traced back to the mid-1800s and a Bible teacher named John Nelson Darby. "He's the culprit," they say, for this allegedly divisive, unsupportable belief.

But is that really the rapture's deepest roots? Or does belief in Jesus' return for His bride go further back than Darby? Do a little digging, and you'll discover that the teaching of the rapture was also prominent among many Puritan preachers in the seventeenth and eighteenth centuries.[3] Keep searching back, and you'll find out that both the early church and the church fathers embraced the belief in Christ's deliverance of the church before the time of tribulation described in Revelation.[4]

Of course, the ultimate litmus test for the legitimacy of any teaching is not a majority vote of theologians in any given century. Rather, the question we must always ask is this: What does the Bible say? If you want to know the truth, *God's* truth, church history can be *helpful*, but grounding a particular belief in Scripture itself is always *essential*.

A Christian radio host once told me (off the air) that it was impossible to find a single verse in the Bible to support the rapture. He is right—there is not a single verse, but rather *many* that speak of this event! They include John 14:1-3; Romans 13:11-12; 1 Corinthians 1:7; 1 Corinthians 15:51-58; 1 Corinthians 16:22; Philippians 3:20; Philippians 4:5; 1 Thessalonians 1:10; 1 Thessalonians 4:13-18; 1 Thessalonians 5:9; 2 Thessalonians 2:6-8; Titus 2:13; James 5:7-8; Hebrews 9:28; Hebrews 10:25; Hebrews 10:37; 1 Peter 1:13; Jude 21; Revelation 3:10; Revelation 3:11; Revelation 22:7; Revelation 22:12; Revelation 22:20.

These are not references to the second coming of Christ, which is a completely different event that will take place some seven years after the rapture (Revelation 19:11-16).

So where does the word *rapture* come from? The English word is a transliteration of the Latin translation of the Greek verb *harpázo.* The Greek term *harpázo* became the Latin *rapiemun* (from *rap-turo*), which translates to the English word *rapture. Harpázo* means "to seize, capture, carry off by force, claim for oneself or suddenly snatch away."[5] Of the 14 times we see this word in the New Testament, every single one refers to something or someone being seized or snatched away. Five times it means "to disappear" or "to be caught up to heaven."[6]

Why Will There Be a Rapture?

It is critical for us as believers to understand that God's anger and wrath toward us was already 100 percent satisfied through Jesus' sacrificial suffering on the cross (Romans 5:8-11; Ephesians 2:3). When our Lord cried, "It is finished!," He was proclaiming that our sin debt was paid in full (John 19:30). When we trust Christ by faith for salvation, God the Father applies Jesus' substitutionary payment for sin to our heavenly account, making us justified and righteous in His sight (Romans 5:1). His suffering while on the cross satisfied God's righteous demands concerning the penalty for sin (Romans 3:23; 6:23; 1 John 2:1-2). As a result, there is now *zero* wrath and condemnation for us—none. That means none now, none during the judgments of the tribulation, none following our death, and none in eternity (Romans 8:1; 1 Thessalonians 1:10; 5:9-10; Revelation 3:10). No wrath. No judgment. It's that simple.

Though we are not promised a carefree life or exemption from sufferings, tribulations, persecutions, or even death, we *are* guaranteed that *God's* fury and wrath will never be poured out upon His bride, the church. He has pledged to nourish and cherish us

(Ephesians 5:29), not blast us with seven years of unimaginable judgments.

When Will the Rapture Occur?

Could we be the "rapture generation"?

As I mentioned earlier, it is impossible for any person to know the exact timing of the rapture. The reason for this is because there is nothing in Scripture that reveals when it will happen. Also, none of us can read the mind of God. He has fixed a moment in time for His Son to return for His bride, and we cannot know that time (Matthew 24:36).

"But wait," you say. "Didn't the writer of Hebrews say that we could 'see the day drawing near'? [10:25]. How does that harmonize with Jesus' words in Acts 1:7, where He told His disciples, 'It is not for you to know times or epochs which the Father has fixed by his own authority'"?

So which is it? Can we see the day drawing near? Or are we forbidden to know the times and seasons leading up to Christ's return? In Acts 1:7, Jesus was referring to His millennial kingdom, not the rapture (Revelation 20:4-6). He did not want His followers to be preoccupied with the physical restoration of Israel's kingdom, as the offer for such a kingdom had already been rejected by the Jewish religious leaders. Christ was now turning His attention toward the birth and establishment of the church (Matthew 16:18; Acts 2–3). Their job was to go back to Jerusalem and wait for the Holy Spirit to indwell them, thus beginning the church age (Acts 1:8; 2:37-47). Similarly, no one alive during the Tribulation will know the day or hour of His second coming either (Matthew 24:36), even though there will be many signs that precede that return (Matthew 24:1-31; Revelation 6-19).

Yet according to Hebrews 10:25, we *can* "see the day drawing near." But if the rapture is a sign-less event, how is it possible for us to see it "drawing near"?

Let's look at it from this perspective:

For many of the events described in Revelation to take place, Israel must be back in its ancient homeland as a nation. As we saw in chapter 7, this has already happened. This fulfilled prophecy is like the first of two "biblical bookends," the other being the collective prophecies presented in Revelation (6–19). What's currently missing in the middle is the rapture. Think of Israel's national rebirth and return to the land as the first of many prophetic "dominoes." The second domino is the rapture, and the third is Antichrist's peace treaty with Israel (Daniel 9:27), which will start the clock ticking on the seven-year tribulation. The other dominoes will be the individual seal, trumpet, and bowl judgments.

According to the pre-tribulational rapture view, before the third domino (Antichrist's peace covenant) can be set into motion, the second domino has to fall (or in this case, be caught up!). Therefore, when we see such compelling evidence that Revelation's prophecies (dominoes) are being set in place *right now*, this tells us we are living in a season when we can "see the day drawing near." Like those far-off mountains my wife and I could see as we approached El Paso, we know these prophecies are on the horizon—we just aren't sure how far away they are.

This doesn't mean someone can know the day, month, year, or even decade in which the rapture will occur. Date-setting (even *decade*-setting) is foolish, arrogant, and unbiblical, and it should *never* be done. Anyone who practices such nonsense is immediately disqualified to speak, teach, or write on the subject of Bible prophecy. However, what we *can* say with a degree of confidence is that we are assuredly living in the last days (2 Timothy 3:1-5; 1 John 2:18) and that we are seeing a prophetic ramping up to the events described in Revelation (that is, the pre-signs we read about in the previous chapter). What we don't know is the length of time that will pass between Israel's birth and the rapture. Christ could call up His bride today. Or in a matter of years. But because of the rebirth of Israel and the stage-setting that is presently taking place, we can certainly say we're living somewhere on the continuum of this prophetic timeline between the two dominoes.

How Will the Rapture Affect the World?

When Jesus snatches us up prior to the unveiling of Antichrist and the start of the tribulation, there will be profound repercussions on Christians, the rest of humanity, and on the planet itself.

Those who are believers will be changed "in a moment, in the twinkling of an eye" (1 Corinthians 15:52). The rapture will happen very quickly. The twinkling of an eye represents about one-tenth of a second, which is faster than a blink. This is as quickly as light reflecting off your eye. Paul describes this as occurring in a "moment" (Greek, *atomo*).[7] In an atomic flash, it will be done. But immediately prior to this, four spectacular things will happen.

1. The Lord Himself will descend with a shout (1 Thessalonians 4:16)

What He declares, no one knows. But perhaps it will be a command summoning forth the resurrections we see later in this same verse. He may say something similar to "Lazarus, come forth" (John 11:43). But whatever His words, they will be authoritative and loud.

2. The voice of the archangel will be heard (4:16)

This will likely be Michael, who is the only archangel named in Scripture, though he is not the only one (Daniel 10:13; Jude 9). Again, we do not know what he will say, but given the occasion, as well as the backdrop of the Jewish wedding custom described in

John 14:1-3, it could be something like the midnight cry of Matthew 25:6: "Behold, the bridegroom! Come out to meet him."

3. The trumpet of God will sound (4:16)

Trumpets were used in the Old Testament to announce the presence of God and to summon the people of God together (Exodus 19:16-19; Numbers 10:1-3). In 1 Corinthians 15:52, Paul calls this the "*last* trumpet," most likely indicating this trumpet blast will occur at the close of the church era (it can't refer to the last trumpet blast *ever* because there will be more trumpets that sound to announce the judgments described in Revelation).

4. The dead in Christ will rise first (4:16)

The bodies of all the believers who have died between Pentecost and this moment will supernaturally come bursting out of their graves, out of the depths of the oceans, all miraculously recomposed. Those now-remade bodies will be reunited with their previously departed spirits descending from heaven. In this way they will take on their glorified state, which will last for all eternity.

After these four things happen, we who are alive at that time will be "caught up" (*harpázo* = "raptured") together with the dead in Christ, where, in the air, we will encounter the Lord Jesus Christ (4:17).

Together, we will all return to heaven, where we will be rewarded at the *bema*, or the judgment seat of Christ (1 Corinthians 3:10-13; 4:5; 2 Corinthians 5:10). It's there that we will remain during the tribulation.

For believers, the rapture is good news. But the same cannot be said for those who are left behind. The coming of Christ for His bride will be as if the earth's very soul has been snatched out of her chest. This spiritually seismic event will send colossal aftershocks reverberating all across the globe in the following ways:

Aftershocks from the Rapture

Moral Aftershocks

After the church is removed, the restraining influence of the Holy Spirit will no longer be present on Earth (2 Thessalonians 2:6-8). It may be difficult to grasp this truth, but along with the preaching of the gospel and the active fight for moral decency, Christians are what's preventing evil from completely overtaking this planet. We are the levy holding back lawlessness—simply by *being here*. The Holy Spirit is holding back evil through our presence and our promotion of goodness and righteousness.

While it's true that things are bad now, the real day of wickedness is yet to come. Today we are witnessing a collective refusal of people to acknowledge God (Romans 1:18-21). This results in blind arrogance (verses 21-23), unprecedented sexual promiscuity (verses 24-25) and perversions (verses 26-27). Culture is presently a breeding ground for the unbridled tolerance, support, participation, and celebration of every kind of sin and evil (verses 28-32). Is it any wonder, then, that three times in Romans 1:21-28, we are told that God "gave them over" to His abandonment wrath? (verses 24, 26, 28)?

If Christians are like salt (which is used to preserve meat and slow the decay process), then what will happen when there is no salt left, as in *not one grain of it* on Earth?[8] Morally speaking, when the rapture occurs, the bottom will drop out. It will be as it was in the days of Noah, with unchecked wickedness and violence, unthinkable sexual perversions, and a whole host of new reasons to hate God (Genesis 6:5-13; Matthew 24:37).

Spiritual Aftershocks

Jesus said we who are Christians are "the light of the world" (Matthew 5:14-16). In the New Testament, light represents the truth and knowledge of God (John 1:4-5; 9:5). Light is also a picture of holiness and righteousness, which is in direct contrast to darkness and sin (1 John 1:5; 3:19). When we are gone, at least initially, there will be no one to speak the truth of God or represent His righteousness. Ours will be a world devoid of *anything* good. Not a single believer in Jesus Christ will breathe Earth's air. Not one. No one will remain to proclaim the truth about sin, salvation, the cross, or eternity. No one will be on hand to light the way to heaven. Like an international power grid failure, there will be a global blackout of truth.

With the salt and light of the world removed, a "deluding influence" sent by God will flood its way into the void (2 Thessalonians 2:11). This will mark the beginning of divine retribution, a direct consequence for refusing to "receive the love of the truth so as to be saved" (2 Thessalonians 2:10). This delusion will ensure that people will continue rejecting God and further believe the lies of Satan, man, and culture. For them, good is evil, and evil is good—very good (Isaiah 5:20). Self is now god, and worshipped as such. We are already seeing the early stages of this delusion all across our country and world today.

Mental and Emotional Aftershocks

Concurrent with this unchecked descent into wickedness will be the emotional meltdown of the masses. Within seconds of the rapture event, billions will experience unparalleled panic, chaos, confusion, and a fear that only those who once clamored for high ground during Noah's flood would have known. The suicide rate will likely skyrocket all over the world.[9] And a tidal wave of mental health issues will send millions into insanity or a mind-numbing world of alcohol and opioids. People will be searching for answers, and yet the deluding influence of God and the inherent deception of their own hearts will lead them to an even darker place inside.

Imagine the personal and psychological effects the rapture will have on people as loved ones are snatched away. Even secularists admit the emotional turmoil associated with that level of human loss cannot possibly be estimated.[10] An instant surge in mental stress, separation anxiety, loss of family members, economic chaos, and all kinds of uncertainty will lead to a host of inconsolable mental and emotional maladies.

There is no way to accurately predict the psychological fallout that will occur as a result of the sudden, unexplainable loss of loved ones—husbands and wives, sons and daughters, and parents and best friends—who have vanished in a flash. Many will become mentally unhinged, while others will suffer nervous breakdowns.

On the flip side of this emotional unravelling will be those who use this departure of believers as an excuse to engage in looting, assault, robbery, violence, and murder. Businesses will suddenly be left vacant and houses abandoned. The lawlessness will be like that experienced in the wake of the anarchist riots of 2020. Godless, decadent criminals will ransack the businesses and homes of those who are snatched away. Possessions once cherished and enjoyed will be repossessed by mobs of thieves. Many will take illegal ownership of cars and guns. Tribal-like warring factions will fight for territories and possession of properties. Disorder, hostility, and nihilism will rule the day.

When false prophet Harold Camping famously predicted the rapture would occur on May 21, 2011, atheists had a field day, setting up Facebook pages and online groups dedicated to "post-rapture looting" and "post-rapture parties."[11] Camping's crazy predictions aside, if that's what atheists are looking forward to, then they won't be disappointed when the real rapture does occur. However, according to Scripture, those parties won't last long, as the Bible prophesies atheism itself will cease to exist in the early days of the tribulation. During this time, the entire world will acknowledge the terrible seal judgments as being from "Him who sits on the throne, and from the wrath of the Lamb" (Revelation 6:16). Yes, atheism will suffer a sudden death after the rapture. Atheists will unexpectedly find themselves believing in God, yet they will also stubbornly refuse to submit to that God.

The Bible also prophesies that many will come to Christ during this time. God will be drawing sinners to salvation, though the price of their faith will be their heads (John 6:44; Revelation 6:9-11; 7:9-14; 13:7-10; 20:4).

Demographic Aftershocks

The aftershocks caused by the rapture will be felt in varying degrees across the world, depending on the concentration of believers in a country. For example, according to the Pew Forum, Yemen, Afghanistan, and other predominantly Muslim countries are less than 1 percent Christian, while nations like the United States and Rwanda have much higher concentrations of believers.[12]

Of course, there is no way to accurately account for how many Christians live in the world because much of the available data is tied to church affiliation (Catholic, Protestant, Orthodox) rather than to individuals. The number of believers raptured in some countries could be in the thousands, while in the United States it could reach into the tens of millions. The current population of the United States is roughly 330 million. So if we were to assume a 10-percent population of Christians, that's 33 million people who would suddenly vanish from the country, not including very young children (possibly as many as 20 million) who are not yet able to understand the gospel or place their faith in Christ for salvation.[13] Again, we cannot know precise numbers, but if these statistics are in the general vicinity, then we could see as many as 50 million people raptured from the United States alone.

At the rapture, America will breathe her last breath as a superpower. Like a person suffering from massive heart failure, she will suddenly and unexpectedly collapse and expire. Some nations around the globe may only become aware of the rapture from the internet or social media because their country's population is minimally affected. Scripture does indicate that during the tribulation, "a great multitude, which no one could count," will be saved, from "every nation and all tribes and peoples and tongues" (Revelation 7:9, 13-14). So, it's conceivable that many of those left behind could know someone who has been raptured. This, too, could be by God's design—as both a witness and a warning to them.

Economic Aftershocks

With the removal of so many people from the planet, jobs will be left unfinished. Mortgages and bills will be unpaid, and with actual and potential homeowners gone, the housing market will collapse, as will Wall Street, now minus millions of individual investors and business employees. The greatest loss for other countries may be in exports, as the United States consumes some 25 percent of the world's goods. However, in countries where Christians do not make up a significant percentage of the buying and selling, the postrapture tremors will have less of an impact.[14] For thoroughly pagan and Islamic nations, the rapture could be like a bump in the road or a bug on the windshield—a temporary annoyance, but hardly noticed.

Paul Ehrlich, a professor at Stanford University, says, "Spread across the globe today, the disappearance of 200 million people (roughly 3 percent of the world's population) might not have major ecological impacts. On the other hand, if the saved were concentrated in America, the effect would be huge."[15]

Political and Geopolitical Aftershocks

After the rapture, governments across the globe will experience upheavals not necessarily due to the number of people missing from their cabinets and other posts, but perhaps more so because of the concentric impact of the rapture's "blast radius" emanating from a superpower like the United States. With anarchy and revolution likely to become rampant, is it possible we could see the US government overturned in a post-rapture America? Will a significant number of key governing figures be taken to heaven from local, state, and federal levels of leadership? Will anarchist groups like Antifa and Black Lives Matter, accompanied by Muslim extremists, storm the White House grounds and other major government buildings nationwide?

Imagine the massive leadership void left behind in Washington, DC, and at the Pentagon. In their place, power-hungry insurgents will rush to seize the reins of government. Political leaders will surely convene in emergency sessions in desperate attempts to keep the ship of state from capsizing and sinking. Other nations—as well as the United Nations itself—will no doubt hold similar crisis meetings. Opportunistic politicians will jockey for position, each one seeking a power grab of their own.

Eventually the dust will settle and one man will have outpaced and out-persuaded all the others. He will posture himself as a peacemaker and display diplomatic skills at a level never before seen. I believe Satan's Antichrist will parlay the post-rapture chaos into his golden ticket, giving him access to the top of the political food chain. He will assemble his ten-nation confederacy as an alliance of nations to rule over Europe. Many nations will suddenly find themselves in dire need of assistance (including America), and thus may form provisional alliances of their own. It is also entirely possible that some governments will simply collapse, afterward suffering violent skirmishes between rogue military contingencies, rebel factions, and tribal coalitions that are all vying for power and control.

Law enforcement in many places will be impotent to hold back angry, riotous, looting, hate-filled hordes. The rule of law may well become a relic of the past.

I write these words being very cognizant of the fact that the United States is not directly mentioned in end-times prophecies. I, therefore, do not intend to overinflate her importance or impact in the context of what will take place following the rapture. I do, however, believe her existence is a force to be reckoned with. When the bride of Christ is taken from her, she will be weakened in ways that cannot be fully predicted or appreciated. And if America does implode as a direct result of the rapture, it will greatly affect the global scene.

Suddenly, like an earthquake that weakens foundations and fortifications, dozens of nations will find themselves vulnerable to attacks from Russia, Iran, China, Islamist regimes, or other enemies. Israel will also be made vulnerable as her greatest and most powerful ally, the United States, reels from the impact of so many missing. Some speculate the Gog and Magog War could take place between the rapture and the signing of Antichrist's covenant with Israel, though it will likely occur after the peace treaty is signed, when Israel is "living securely" in the land (Ezekiel 38:8, 11, 14).

A World Without Christians

Think about this: In the moment that immediately follows the rapture, not a single human on planet Earth will be a believer in

Jesus Christ. Not one. In the twinkling of an eye, the world will be changed instantly, with America suddenly being transformed from the land of the free to the domain of the damned.

> For believers, the rapture will represent deliverance. But for those left behind, it will spell doom and devastation.

All this highlights the reality that when God removes His restraining influence on sin, that alone will represent a devastating judgment on planet Earth (2 Thessalonians 2:6-7). Of course, conditions could turn out to be a lot worse than what I have described here. Past disasters and crises will pale in comparison to that which is coming. For believers, the rapture will represent deliverance. But for those left behind, it will spell doom and devastation. We will finally experience our long-awaited hope of heaven, while the rest of the world experiences a frustrating hell on Earth.

How Might the Rapture Be Explained?

As mentioned earlier, the immediate effects of the rapture will vary from country to country, yet the entire world will be affected. Attempts to explain what has just taken place will undoubtedly flood in from a wide variety of sources—governments, scientists, philosophers, and major news outlets. Initially, social media will explode as every account holder suddenly becomes an "expert." Fake news will rise to a whole new level as opinions, ideas, theories, conspiracies, pictures, and dramatic video footage consume virtually every feed and thread. If the rapture were to occur today, Twitter, Facebook, and Instagram would likely crash from the unprecedented numbers of simultaneous posts. What will people be saying? How will they explain our departure?

With darkened minds, of course.

Devoid of the knowledge of God, those left behind will be left to their own futile speculations (Romans 1:21; Ephesians 4:17). We are currently living in an age when people will believe virtually anything they are told. But in that day, what will they believe is the cause of our sudden disappearance? Alien abductions? An atmospheric anomaly? An undetected wormhole? No doubt with billions of people weighing in, no theory will be off limits.

But consider this: Revelation tells us that not long after this event the whole earth will acknowledge the seal and bowl judgments as being from "Him who sits on the throne, and from the wrath of the Lamb" (Revelation 6:15-17; 16:9, 11, 21; 19:19). This makes it conceivable that those who remain here may well "get it right," attributing the sudden disappearance of all Christians to Jesus and His rapture. But keep in mind that a grand delusion will also descend upon humanity at this time (2 Thessalonians 2:10-12). In other words, as it relates to the rapture, it is possible people will know this event was caused by God but not know *why*. It is also likely that, due to their inherently darkened minds and God-sent delusion, they *will* know, but they won't even care!

The prince of the power of the air will ensure that this global news event is manipulated and spun in such a way as to conform to the narrative that best serves his Antichrist's soon-to-be-revealed agenda. False prophets and spiritual gurus will also arise immediately, deceiving millions online and in the streets and accumulating followers, just as Jesus prophesied in Matthew 24:4-5, 11. It is also entirely reasonable to imagine that the truth about what has just happened could be suppressed or even deleted by the lords of social media, perhaps in an effort to downplay the impact and significance of the disappearance of countless millions.

Candlelight vigils for the missing could rapidly be replaced with celebrations, perhaps a foreshadowing of the way humanity will celebrate the deaths of God's two witnesses a few years later (Revelation 11:7-10). In that spirit, these "rapture parties" could early on become a sort of "good riddance" to those annoying Christians, and also a way to get "real estate and cheap cars."[16]

Because of the immediate need to ensure their own survival, large numbers of people may quickly lose interest in the rapture or why it occurred. Reports of the event could quickly fade to the back page or out of the news altogether.

And Satan's misdirection campaign will be in full swing.

As happened with other world catastrophes, after the rapture, many people will reach the point of wanting to move on with life. Strategies will soon be proposed to help them recover and move forward. Satan will seize this opportunity to divert humanity's attention toward a rising figure in global politics, one who is said to be working on a solution to relieve the adverse aftershocks of the rapture and bring peace to the Middle Eastern nations.

The $64,000 Question

By this time I am guessing you may be feeling a stirring within your heart—both a longing to be snatched away by the Bridegroom as well as a burden for those who will be left behind. In all this, you may even be wondering, *Why is God waiting? What's the big holdup?*

Here are three biblically grounded answers that can help us understand God's potential motivations for delaying the blessed hope.

1. God is not finished preparing the stage for the end-times drama (Revelation 6–19). As we saw in chapter 7, emerging foreshocks are now indicating the perhaps soon arrival of Revelation's prophecies. Those prophecies-in-formation let us know we are living in the last days. God's sovereign plan

for the ages is unfolding in stages. While this doesn't postpone the rapture in any way, it does show us He is putting things in place in accordance with His preordained plan and perfect timing.

2. God is preparing the last Gentile to be saved. As a nation, Israel's rejection of the Messiah caused a "partial hardening…*until* the fullness of the Gentiles has come in" (11:25). The last Gentile, then, is the final person on Earth who will believe in Christ for salvation and be added to the church, the bride of Christ. I believe either at the moment this person confesses faith in Jesus, or very shortly afterward, our Lord will descend from heaven with a shout, initiating the rapture (1 Thessalonians 4:16). God's waiting has to do with His great patience toward sinners, giving them the opportunity to repent and to be saved (2 Peter 3:9).

3. God is preparing His bride to meet her Bridegroom (Romans 13:11-14). Jesus wants His beloved to be holy and blameless at His appearing (Ephesians 5:26-27). To do this, she must first wake up (Revelation 3:2) and then purify herself for her Lord (1 John 3:1-3). Are you prepared? More about this in chapter 10.

Rest assured, the rapture will not be hastened or delayed by even one second. It will arrive right on time and in accordance with God's prophetic design. He is counting down the days, hours, and minutes that are known only to Him.

Some accuse Christians of using the rapture as some sort of scare tactic to frighten people into believing in Jesus. I suppose you could say the same thing of Noah as he preached about the coming flood. And yet the Bible doesn't call him a fearmonger, but a "preacher of righteousness" (2 Peter 2:5). Others claim that by speaking or teaching about the rapture, we are purposefully being overly sensational and dramatic. But considering the disorientation, devastation, destruction, and damnation that will occur immediately following this event, that actually might not be a bad accusation. So yes, there's a sense in which we are sensational and dramatic. And that is by God's design. Like a massive ark rising on the plain, the more we talk of the rapture, the more people can see the open door to Him who alone can deliver them "from the wrath to come" (1 Thessalonians 1:10).

In the meantime, Jesus' bride is to maintain an eager and expectant hope concerning the rapture (1 Corinthians 1:7; Philippians 3:20). We are to be "looking for the blessed hope and the appearing of our great God and Savior, Christ Jesus" (Titus 2:13). I suppose few understand this expectant longing better than a bride-to-be. Her wedding day is the moment she has dreamed about all her life. It has preoccupied her mind since the day her beloved proposed to her. And the closer she sees the day drawing near, the greater her anticipation and excitement grow.

Sadly, the bride of Christ has lost that sense of eager anticipation. We rarely even talk about our "wedding day" anymore when we gather. And some have denied its existence altogether.

But wouldn't it be beautifully inspiring if everyone reading these words renewed that spirit of hope within his or her heart? And imagine how much joy it would bring to Jesus' own heart if His beloved bride once again began looking forward to the day when she will be His!

May your soul be filled with the wonder of His love for you, and may you be captivated by a longing to see Him in the clouds, perhaps soon!

Chapter 9

BE STILL AND KNOW THAT I AM GOD

I t's no secret that mankind has advanced more in the last 100 years than in all previous centuries combined. Progress and achievements in science, travel, medicine, communications, and technology have accelerated beyond what anyone could have imagined or predicted. We have ascended to the pinnacle of progress. We have crowned ourselves with glory and grandeur, reveled in our accomplishments, and revered ourselves with near-godlike status.

And yet, as recent history has demonstrated, we are also surprisingly fragile and frail. Like a house of cards, humanity is perpetually but one step away from global chaos and collapse. In a brief moment, a lone assassin propelled the nations into World War I. On 9/11, a handful of Islamic terrorists forever changed history. An isolated weather event can bring a country's citizens to the brink of despair. An unexpected downturn in the stock market can threaten to cripple an entire economy. A single rocket can undo decades of peaceful coexistence, thrusting nations into years of bloody conflict.

And one invisible virus can shut down the planet.

If recent events have taught us anything, it's that the things upon which we depend daily can turn on us in a heartbeat. At any given moment, humanity's finger flirts precariously close to the panic button, and with a solitary nudge, we are propelled into yet another era of global chaos.

Yes, we humans are a peculiar race. We have grown more aware that within a few days, weeks, or even minutes, everything as we know it can all come crashing down around us. The physical and financial fallout from global disasters, whether they be natural or man-made, can be devastating.

The Explosion of Fear

But ultimately, life is measured in more than dollars and dividends. Upon reflection, the most severe aftershocks of such catastrophes are the emotional, mental, and relational ones that accompany them. When major calamities reverberate across the globe, it is people who suffer, not just economies and spreadsheets.

Such was the case with the ongoing effects of the COVID-19 pandemic. While many people appear to have adjusted and remain relatively stable on the surface, much of the damage done remains hidden under the rubble. The effects of long-term quarantine mandates sent most of the world into a subconscious trauma. By way of example, when a person survives a near-fatal car crash, it takes time for the bruises, soreness, and chronic pain to kick in. In the wake of the coronavirus event, more than half (58 percent) of Americans reported a heightened sense of worry and stress related to the outbreak.[1] This led to excess side-effects, including overeating, sleeplessness, excessive drinking, drug abuse, headaches, stomach disorders, and anger. Some suicide hotlines received as much as a 60-percent spike in their call volume.

These kinds of effects can take an extended toll on the mental health of individuals, communities, and beyond, nearly always producing increased depression, PTSD, substance abuse, domestic violence, child abuse, crime, and other mental and behavioral disorders.

Beneath all of what was taking place on the surface, hidden from friends and Facebook feeds, flowed a subterranean river of *fear*. As we navigated this unparalleled disruption of our way of life, all kinds of fears exploded forth like a volcanic eruption and sent lava flows of apprehension and anxiety cascading down into virtually every country and community worldwide. It didn't take long for the lava to ignite fires that spread, scorching everything that once defined us as a culture.

Fear of contracting the virus.

Fear of not wearing a mask.

Fear of others not wearing masks.

Fear of those who coughed in public.

Fear of contamination from touching objects.

Fear of people closer than six feet to us.

Fear of reduced immunities from being quarantined.

Fear of continued isolation.

Fear of delayed education.

Fear of travel.

Fear of lost or reduced income.

Fear of being furloughed or fired.

Fear of sporting events.

Fear of gathering for church.

Fear of a second or third wave of outbreaks.

Fear of the future.

Fear of the unknown.

No single fear threatens to steal our sanity or wreck our emotional stability, but combined, the fears slowly chip away at us, diminishing our mental and emotional strength. From a human perspective, this "fear between the ears" can be the lone voice in our head that perpetually inspires negative thoughts and emotions. And in some instances, it can even take over our souls.

While it can be argued that some of the aforementioned anxieties were fully warranted, the line between justifiable concern and irrational phobia can, at times, be almost indiscernible—especially when the number of reasons for fear become overwhelming.

Going forward, what does all this mean for those of us who follow Jesus Christ? What is *our* personal and corporate response to such crises? How can we be different, if at all? Are we inherently insulated from such emotional contagions? Or are we like everyone else, vulnerable to being held captive by the same fears that plague the rest of humanity? How can we cultivate discernment and display courage in an age filled with so much anxiety?

The answers to these questions cannot be found within ourselves, but only in God. Our solution is not scientific, but scriptural. God's truth shows us when to be cautious and when to forge ahead with confidence. It's not about being reckless, careless, or "mocking the storm." And it's not about putting God to the test by justifying irresponsible behavior. Rather it's something much more intelligent, more theological.

And more sacred.

Because of our proximity to the fulfillment of Bible prophecy and Satan's ongoing strategy to destroy and enslave humanity, national and global crises like the ones we're seeing today are likely to increase in frequency in the days ahead. Therefore, our response must be measured and motivated solely by the unchanging hope that is found in God's Word alone. It is there that we find both our survival and our spiritual sanity are rooted in the person of God Himself.

> With Scripture as our guide, though the whole world
> around us may be coming apart, we won't be.

Navigating a Crisis

Turning to an ancient psalm, we discover the truth and wisdom necessary to navigate any crisis we may face in these last days, whether they be personal or global. Scripture is *the* key to maintaining structural integrity in our emotions and spirit during emergencies and in times of distress and uncertainty. With Scripture as our guide, though the whole world around us may be coming apart, we won't be.

Psalm 46 was written during the reign of King Hezekiah in 701 BC. Sennacherib, king of Assyria, was preparing to lay siege to Jerusalem, the capital of the southern kingdom of Judah. The northern kingdom of Israel had already been taken captive (2 Kings 17; 18:13–19:37). In an attempt to placate the Assyrian ruler, King Hezekiah sent an offering of silver and gold from both the house of the Lord and the king's personal treasury (2 Kings 18:13-16). When the count was completed, he had gathered 360,000 ounces of silver and 36,000 ounces of gold, totaling roughly $79 million by today's standards. But despite this massive payoff, Sennacherib didn't bat an eye. Instead, he sent his army onward to Jerusalem.

And his terms to the people of Judah? Make peace with the Assyrian king, and he promises you will "eat each of his vine and each of his fig tree and drink each of the waters of his own cistern" (verse 31). Further, Judah's inhabitants were assured they would be taken away to a "land of grain and new wine, a land of bread and vineyards, a land of olive trees and honey." And, oh yes—"you may [get to] live and not die" (verse 32). By contrast, the godless despot had earlier stated that if Judah's inhabitants continued defending their city, Jerusalem, they would be "doomed to eat their own dung and drink their own urine" (verse 27). Nice.

Providential Provision

Upon hearing this less-than-promising proclamation, King Hezekiah immediately sought God in prayer. He also sent a representative to the prophet Isaiah, who responded, "Do not be afraid because of the words that you have heard, with which the servants of the king of Assyria have blasphemed Me" (19:6). And with that encouragement, Hezekiah continued praying, acknowledging the Lord's sovereignty over the futile Syrian gods (19:15-19). Further, he prayed earnestly for Jerusalem's deliverance, such that "all the kingdoms of the earth may know that You alone, LORD, are God" (19:19).

Imagine for a moment being a resident of Judah during this time of national fear and uncertainty. You're about to be attacked, conquered, and led off into captivity by a powerful pagan king. Or you'll be brutally killed. Either way, your future isn't looking too bright.

It is in this context that a group of men known as the sons of Korah penned what has become one of the most beloved of all psalms. In it we are given a unique perspective on crisis that transforms our minds, realigns our emotions, and infuses our hearts with comfort, strength, and hope. This psalm begins by boldly declaring,

> God is our refuge and strength,
> A very present help in trouble (46:1).

These words paint a beautiful portrait of our God, first describing Him as our "refuge," the ultimate place of security. The Hebrew word translated "refuge" (*maseh*) means "shelter from danger." For Judah, this meant a literal, physical danger. David similarly wrote,

"In the day of trouble He will conceal me in his tabernacle; in the secret place of His tent *He will hide me*; He will lift me up on a rock" (Psalm 27:5; cf. Psalm 14:6). God being our fortress of protection is a repeated theme throughout the Old Testament (Psalms 61:3; 62:7, 8; 71:7; 73; 28; 91:2, 9; 94:22; 142:5; Isaiah 25:4; Jeremiah 17:17; Joel 3:16). This fortress of retreat in Him is impregnable, His safety more than just a comforting feeling. Instead, it's a *reality*! Nothing can touch us while we're in the place of His refuge. Only a force greater than Elohim ("the Strong One") could penetrate this protective shelter, for "if God is for us, who is against us?" (Romans 8:31).

Psalm 46:1 tells us that, in seasons of peril, we have no reason to panic as others do. We do not look to political leaders or government for relief from anxiety or deliverance out of perilous times. Nor do we rely on human relationships or look within for our peace. Instead, we run to *God*.

It is also in this refuge that we find a supernatural source of "strength." Alone, we are helpless. And even with others, we remain vulnerable to fear and failure. However, with God as our refuge, we discover a strength far beyond what this world, or our own willpower, can provide. It is a heavenly supply, one that is never depleted. When circumstances are at their darkest, we must first seek shelter in the refuge of our Redeemer.

This psalm goes on, further describing this great God of ours, declaring Him as "a very present help in time of trouble" (verse 1). In other words, though deliverance from tribulation may be delayed, His sustaining support during such times does not. It is never late, and always sufficient, "a *very present* help." This means God's provision is *enough* for any situation we may face. It means *He* is sufficient.

But is He, practically speaking? Did the psalm writers really intend to communicate such certainty of peace and comfort? Or are they merely waxing poetic here? Can we ever attain this level of confidence and strength? Is that even possible? Was Psalm 46 written merely as some sort of philosophical platitude meant to medicate our emotions? Are these words nothing more than a mental exercise, mind trick, or emotional exercise meant to help divert our minds away from our problems? Or was it penned in real time and during an actual national crisis? Could it be *truth*, God's truth, that when received, effectually relieves us of *all* our fears and anxieties?

What if things today get worse? What if evil and lawlessness were to exponentially increase in our culture? What if the persecution of believers were to ramp up and become intense? What if new pathogens are unleashed into the mainstream of society? What if governmental authorities increase their unjust overreach into our public and private lives? What if the times in which we are living become even more volatile and uncertain? What if global catastrophes and upheavals were to multiply in number? What then?

Korah's sons anticipated our questions and respond with this:

> Therefore we will not fear, though the earth should change
>> And though the mountains slip into the heart of the sea;
> Though its waters roar and foam,
>> Though the mountains quake at its swelling pride (verses 2-3).

Can you envision a greater disaster than the entire Earth's topography being moved out of its place? Can you picture something more alarming and dreadful than the mountains collapsing and crumbling into the sea? Imagine the tsunami-like aftershocks that would result from such seismic shifts. Earth is our home, but if the earth itself is radically rearranged below and all around us, what would we do? What *could* we do?

"Even if all that were to happen," God says, "there is *still* no need for you to fear." Why? Because of what you just heard about God being your refuge.

Blessed Assurance

And now for the challenge: The degree of difficulty at which you are able to fully embrace this scriptural truth is a revealing sign of how well you have come to know your God. Do you get it? David did, and it prompted him to declare,

> The LORD is my light and my salvation;
>> Whom shall I fear?
> The LORD is the defense of my life;
>> Whom shall I dread?
> When evildoers came upon me to devour my flesh,
> My adversaries and my enemies, they stumbled and fell.
> Though a host encamp against me,
>> My heart will not fear;
> Though war arise against me,
>> In spite of this I shall be confident (Psalm 27:1-3).

"In spite of this."

Does this not beautifully describe life's greatest challenges and struggles? Though the earth should change…though the mountains slip into the sea…though its waters roar and foam…though the mountains quake…though evildoers come upon me…though adversaries, enemies, even a *host* of them surround me…

Or paint your own scenario. Look back at your past. Scan your present. Imagine your worst future. Now insert them *all* into this psalm. "Though _____ should happen to me, every one of them…all at the same time—in spite of this…"

I. Will. *Not.* Fear.

And again, why? One reason: Because God, *the* God, *my* God—the sovereign and supreme One—is my very present help in my times of trouble.

Our ability to exercise this kind of confidence is ultimately based upon whether we are building our lives on rock or on sand. In Matthew 7, after explaining the two roads of life, the two destinies, and the danger of phony faith, Jesus concludes,

> Everyone who hears these words of Mine and acts on them, may be compared to a wise man who built his house on the rock. And the rain fell, and the floods came, and the winds blew and slammed against that house; and yet it did not fall, for it had been founded on the rock. Everyone who hears these words of Mine and does not act on them, will be like a foolish man who built his house on the sand. The rain fell, and the floods came, and the winds blew and slammed against that house; and it fell—and great was its fall (Matthew 7:24-27).

As we learned in chapter 1, adversity is the great revealer. When a crisis hits, we find out what we're really made of. And it's sometimes on display for others to see as well. Adversity unmasks us, revealing how sound and secure our faith is. And why would it be so critically important that your life is built on the rock? Simple.

Because of what's coming.

Brace for Impact

In the blockbuster movie *Taken*, actor Liam Neeson plays Bryan Mills, an ex-CIA operative who is also father to his semi-estranged teenage daughter (Kim). While visiting Paris with a friend, kidnappers break into Kim's apartment and begin abducting her friend. Terrified and crying, Kim calls her dad and explains the situation. Mills instructs her to quickly find a bedroom, hide under a bed, and then to tell him when she's there. While the intruders violently ransack the apartment searching for her, Kim frantically scrambles under the bed, whispering on the phone to her father that she made it there.

Mills pauses, contemplating the gravity of what he is about to tell his daughter.

And in what is arguably the most gut-wrenching moment of the movie, he then informs her that she is going to be taken.

Friend, I wish I could tell you that our world is getting better. That evil will abate and righteousness will rise. I wish I could tell you that if you are nice and neighborly to non-Christians, they will respect you, love you, and miraculously come to Christ. I wish I could tell you that if you stand uncompromisingly for God's truth, values, and morality, culture will applaud and support you. But I can't tell you those things because it's not the picture Scripture paints for our future. This is not the world we live in.

On the contrary, Jesus explicitly warned us,

> If the world hates you, you know that it has hated Me before it hated you. If you were of the world, the world would love its own; but because you are not of the world, but I chose you out of the world, because of this the world hates you. Remember the word that I said to you, "A slave is not greater than his master." If they persecuted Me, they will also persecute you; if they kept My word, they will keep yours also. But all these things they will do to you for My name's sake, because they do not know the One who sent me (John 15:18-21).

All mankind is broken, desperate, evil, and racing like a runaway train toward a collision course with Revelation. The present spirit of Antichrist, along with rampant godlessness, ever-increasing immorality, and emerging last-days prophecies gives us every reason to believe that more tough days lie ahead. More unknown threats. And that future crises and challenges await us.

But rather than crumble within or capitulate to fear, your first response must always be to run to the Refuge. Through practice, you must develop a spiritual instinct that *trusts* over trying. A faith that waits on Him instead of worrying about your circumstances. As you journey on a path filled with danger and surrounded by darkness, you must choose to reject the fear that would intimidate and paralyze others. No matter what the world, life, others, or self may say.

"In spite of this…"

Peace in the Presence

And regardless of how Satan may tempt, accuse, or attack you, even then—*especially* then—you will not fear simply because God is with you. He is your calm within the fury of the storm. His relational presence is the very essence of your joy and is at the core of your comfort. This enduring divine presence was also at the heart of Christ's mission to restore a rebellious, sin-stained humanity back to the unhindered communion it once experienced with Him in the garden.

This is why Jesus chose His disciples—"that they would *be with Him*" (Mark 3:14).

Being with Him is also one of His motivations in returning for us, taking us to the Father's house so that "where I am, there *you may be also*" (John 14:3).

Remember what Jesus asked of the Father in His high priestly prayer on the night before His crucifixion? He implored, "Father, I desire that they also, whom You have given Me, *be with Me where I am*" (John 17:24).

We see this as well in one of Jesus' last promises, which He gave prior to His ascension: "Lo, *I am with you always*, even to the end of the age" (Matthew 28:20; see also Hebrews 13:5-6).

This assurance is also purposefully embedded within one of the major prophecies about the rapture. After being caught up into the clouds to meet the Lord in the air, "we shall always *be with the Lord*" (1 Thessalonians 4:17).

And it's one of God's most precise promises about heaven: "I heard a loud voice from the throne, saying, 'Behold, the *tabernacle of God is among men*, and He will *dwell among them*, and they shall be His people, and *God Himself will be among them*'" (Revelation 21:3).

Living in God's presence! I ask you: Could there be anything better?

His *presence* is your ultimate peace.

As happened with Shadrach, Meshach, and Abednego, there will always be the presence of a "fourth" in the fire with you (Daniel 3:24-25). No matter how hot the flame, He stands and walks with you. Indeed, nothing can separate a Christian from the love and presence of his or her God.

Not tribulation nor distress.

Not persecution nor famine.

Not nakedness nor peril, nor death by the sword.

No angel or devil possesses the power to take away His presence. No present circumstance can remove it. No future calamity can rob you of it. No earthly authority can forbid it. No distance or loneliness can threaten it. No created thing can subvert it. And nothing in this life, or in the next—and not even death itself—"will be able to separate us from the love of God, which is in Christ Jesus our Lord" (Romans 8:35-39).

Even if we face persecution and martyrdom for our faith, "in all these things we overwhelmingly conquer through Him who loved us" (verse 37).

In other words, no matter what happens, you win! You were born again to conquer and overcome the sins and struggles of this life. Despite what the devil hurls *at* you, and regardless of what the world does *to* you, defeat is not in your future because of God's presence and present help in your life!

On the contrary, it is those without Christ who crumble beneath the weight of human tragedy. The best refuge into which they can retreat is human relationships, or the fragile mental and emotional fortresses they have constructed within themselves. When tragedy strikes, many predictably spiral into a black hole of despair, depression, and fear, leading some to become lost in a haze of alcoholic or narcotic nothingness.

Let It Go

Indeed, the earth does appear to be shifting beneath our feet. And humanity is desperately scrambling for solid ground. But there is no terra firma for them. No refuge. No help, present or future. And therefore, no hope. Unless they repent.

But that which was available to Judah's sons and daughters in 701 BC is accessible to you right now. Psalm 46 reminded them that despite the very real threat of invasion and kidnapping, God was still their "stronghold" (verses 7, 11), which is a fascinating Hebrew word, meaning "a secure, high retreat."[2] The word is used 15 times in the Old Testament, nearly always referring to the Lord Himself (2 Samuel 22:3; Psalms 9:10; 18:3; 46:7, 11; 59:10; Isaiah 33:16). It describes a well-protected place too high for ordinary climbers to access and elevated beyond the reach of would-be attackers. It is a safe, fortified location. Therefore, those who take refuge there are removed from danger. The word is clear: God is our secure, safe, and high retreat from physical, emotional, and spiritual enemies.

For Hezekiah, his comfort would also be strengthened in knowing that Jerusalem, the "city of God," would remain "the holy dwelling places of the Most High" (Psalm 46:4). He was assured, along with the rest of Judah, that God was still "in the midst of her," and that He would help her "when morning dawns" (the presumed hour of attack, verse 5). Despite the uproar of the nations, the psalmists reaffirmed the reality that "the LORD of hosts is with us; the God of Jacob is our stronghold" (verse 7 ESV).

Again, His *presence*. God alone has the power to "make wars [threats, dangers, crises] to cease" (verse 9). Because of this, the people of Judah believed His sovereignty could end the devastation that troubled and threatened them.

What was Judah to do in response to these truths about God in light of the crisis they were facing? Were they to run? Escape? Panic? Defend themselves? Fight?

None of the above. Rather, they were admonished, "Cease striving and know that I am God" (verse 10).

In other translations, verse 10 is rendered as "Be still." The Hebrew word used here means "to relax" or "let go" (literally, "let sink"). It means to exhale, be calm, don't carry the burden yourself. Instead, drop it. Surrender the anxiety. Stop striving in your own energy and strength. Give it all to God. Just…

Let it go.

By the way, this was not some suggestive helpful hint for happy living, or a pathway to a better self. Rather, this was a command from God. A divine directive. As believers, God doesn't give us the options of worrying or being anxious, both of which should be foreign concepts to us (Matthew 6:25-26, 28, 31, 34; Luke 10:41; 12:11, 22). Instead, we are to cast our burdens, big and small, on the Lord, delivering all our anxiety at His doorstep (Psalm 55:22; Philippians 4:6-7; 1 Peter 5:7).

This is why the author of Hebrews encourages us to "confidently say, 'The Lord is my helper, I will not be afraid. What shall man do to me?'" (13:6).[3]

The clear application is that we possess the ability to stop stressing, worrying, or fearing over what might, could, or will happen.

As we release that burden in our minds, replacing it with His unchangeable, incontrovertible truth, we will cease striving and *know* that He is God. "Know" here (Hebrew, *yāda'*) means to *experientially* encounter something or someone. It is a very intimate term used in Scripture to refer to the knowledge God possesses, our ability to know good and evil, and even physical intimacy in marriage (Genesis 3:5, 7, 22; 4:1).

Far beyond trite words on a plaque or a posted meme and deeper than some Christian catchphrase, the command to "be still and know I am God" should become part of our abiding mindset. It is a truth we should weave into our hearts, into the very fabric of our faith, into the practical DNA of our daily lives.

Knowing He is God means thinking, believing, and living in such a way that His sovereign control over all things drives out our panic over and preoccupation with what's happening out there in the world or in our hearts.

> Challenging days are ahead. But God has history, the whole world, and you in His hands.

Maybe you've never felt the earth move beneath your feet. Then again, maybe you have. Maybe you've felt your whole world crumbling all around you. And if you've paid attention, you've also seen whole countries buckling beneath the strain of various crises. Billions of people are desperately reaching out for something solid to grab on to. When businesses are lost, economies are upended, governments are scrambling for answers, and everyone is wondering, "What's next?"

It's very likely that what happened in 2020 is the tip of the iceberg. Challenging days are ahead. But God has history, the whole world, and you in His hands. He is your refuge and your present help and stronghold. His enduring presence comforts and protects you. Though we have to live on this earth, we can also rise above it, soaring with wings like eagles (Isaiah 40:31).

Your job in the midst of all that is taking place is to relax, let go, not fear, and acknowledge Him as God. When new pandemics and perils come, you must choose to firmly place your trust in Him.

After all, that's what faith is.

So whatever happened with Sennacherib's planned invasion of Jerusalem? In answer to Hezekiah's prayer, and before the Assyrian army had a chance to shoot a single arrow, the angel of the Lord showed up and slew 185,000 soldiers *in one night* (2 Kings 19:32-37; Isaiah 37:36). As for Sennacherib himself, he returned home to Nineveh, and while worshipping in the temple of his god, two of his sons entered, killing him with a sword (2 Kings 19:36-37; Isaiah 37:37-38). There would be no refuge or stronghold for the king who dared attack God's city and God's people.

And God's people and Jerusalem survive to this day.

Chapter 10

OUR FINEST HOUR

n his autobiography *Just as I Am*, legendary evangelist Billy Graham recounted an unforgettable conversation he had with President John F. Kennedy shortly after his election.

> On the way back to the Kennedy house, the president-elect stopped the car and turned to me. "Do you believe in the Second Coming of Jesus Christ?" he asked.
>
> "I most certainly do."
>
> "Well, does my church believe it?" Kennedy inquired.
>
> "They have it in their creeds," I replied.
>
> "They don't preach it," he said. "They don't tell us much about it. I'd like to know what you think."
>
> I explained what the Bible said about Christ coming the first time, dying on the cross, rising from the dead, and then promising that he would come back again. "Only then," I said, "are we going to have permanent world peace."
>
> "Very interesting," he said, looking away. "We'll have to talk more about that someday." And he drove on.

Several years later, the two met again, this time at the 1963 National Prayer Breakfast. Graham wrote:

> I had the flu. After I gave my short talk, and he gave his, we walked out of the hotel to his car together, as was always our custom. At the curb, he turned to me.
>
> "Billy, could you ride back to the White House with me? I'd like to see you for a minute."
>
> "Mr. President, I've got a fever," I protested. "Not only am I weak, but I don't want to give you this thing. Couldn't we wait and talk some other time?"
>
> It was a cold, snowy day, and I was freezing as I stood there without my overcoat.
>
> "Of course," he said graciously.

Sadly, the president and the preacher would never meet again. Later that year, Kennedy was assassinated in Dallas. Graham comments, "His hesitation at the car door, and his request, haunt me still. What was on his mind? Should I have gone with him? It was an irrecoverable moment."[1]

An irrecoverable moment. And a missed opportunity.

The Silent Hammer

Graham's encounter with the president illustrates a life principle—a spiritual law, really. And it's this: Some moments are like doors. They open briefly, and then they close, sometimes permanently. A fleeting opportunity can be captured or it can be lost forever. We see this life principle tragically portrayed during the days of Noah. The door to his massive ark remained open throughout the entire time the boatbuilder heralded God's truth to his generation. Day after day, Noah pounded wood and preached righteousness. Though we are not told of his specific words, we can assume that he, like Billy Graham, kept his message focused on the essentials.

You are a sinner.

God's judgment is coming.

He has provided one way out, a way of deliverance and escape.

You must repent and seek refuge inside His ark of salvation.

We can be sure he spoke to those who came to gawk at or mock "Noah's Folly." Maybe he took regular trips to town for supplies, speaking to those who would ask him, "Why are you building such a monstrosity?" It's conceivable he paused to preach formal sermons on certain days of the week. Or perhaps he made sacrifices to his God openly and regularly as a testimony to all that a blood sacrifice is necessary for sin. Or he could have done all the above. But no matter his schedule, methods, or specific words, Noah kept at it. God's prophesied deluge was coming and though Noah may not have been privy to the month or the hour, he did realize his time was limited. The clock was ticking. Turns out he was given around 75 years, a mere blip on eternity's timeline.[2]

Then the day finally arrived. Noah's well-worn hammer lay silent on the ground. His pitch bucket was empty. His saw had done its job. He and his family entered the ark, and God Himself shut the door (Genesis 7:16). One week passed. And I wonder if, during those seven days, anyone noticed the echoes of construction work had strangely stopped. Did those who had mocked him realize his project was now complete? Were they aware they had heard the last sermon of their lives?

Now safely inside, Noah would no longer be preaching to his generation. No more pleading with his neighbors or pointing them toward the ark for salvation. No more time to be God's witness to a godless world.

And then the rains came.

The day of judgment had arrived. And the Spirit who had waited patiently would strive no more with man (Genesis 6:3). Noah knew this moment would one day come. He could observe the progress of the ark's construction. And the longer he labored, the closer the hour of reckoning drew near.

What's in a Name?

Though Noah was not given the precise day God's prophecy would be fulfilled, he was given a clue about it through a most peculiar means—not through direct revelation or a supernatural sign, but rather, through a man's *name*. Noah's grandfather was Methuselah, the person famously remembered for living longer than any other human being. At 969 years old, Methuselah holds the record for the longest life ever, a record that has never been broken. However, as it turns out, the measure of this man's days was overshadowed by the meaning of his name. In Hebrew, *Methuselah* means, "when he is gone, it will come" (or "when he is gone, it shall be sent"). What will come? What shall be sent? What is the "it" here? Scripture gives us another clue in Genesis 7:11-12:

> In the six hundredth year of Noah's life, in the second month, on the seventeenth day of the month, on the same day all the fountains of the great deep burst open, and the floodgates of the sky were opened. The rain fell upon the earth for forty days and forty nights.

This is where a little math comes in handy, so hang with me.

- Methuselah was 187 years old when his son, Lamech (Noah's father), was born.
- Lamech was 182 years old when Noah was born.
- The flood came in the six hundredth year of Noah's life.

So when Noah was born, his grandfather, Methuselah, was 369

years old (187 + 182 = 369). *Exactly* 600 years later, the flood came (Genesis 7:6, 11).

That is, 600 + 369 = 969, or the year Methuselah died.

Therefore, Methuselah's name signifies that when *he* (Methuselah) is gone, *it* (the flood) will come.

Though Scripture tells us the specific month and day the great flood came, we are *not* told that Methuselah actually died on the seventeenth. But what if both his death and the flood coincided to the *day*? What if, upon closing his eyes for the last time (presumably dying of extreme old age!) the first raindrops fell from the sky, triggering the event that would send billions to a watery grave? What if, upon exhaling his final breath on his bed, the great fountains of the deep exploded with violent geysers shooting up into the sky? Or could his death have activated the closing of the ark's door one week prior to the flood event?

Because Bible prophecies are always filled with precision, even to the day, why not this one as well?

What we can know for certain was that while Methuselah was alive, he was a living billboard—a walking, breathing, bearded sermon. As long as he walked the earth, God would hold off global judgment. As long as there was breath in his lungs, people had time to repent and be saved. As long as Methuselah was among them, the door of the ark remained open.

A.W. Pink writes, "A divine revelation was memorialized in his name. The world was to last as long as this son of Enoch lived."[3]

No Excuse

Do you see the patience and grace of God on display here? The ark's open door represented the opportunity of salvation. This same longsuffering is what Peter was talking about in 1 Peter 3:19-20, writing that Christ (through Noah) "went and made proclamation to the spirits now in prison, who once were disobedient when the patience of God kept waiting in the days of Noah, during the construction of the ark."

God's patience had actually been demonstrated much earlier, hundreds of years before Noah felled his first tree. Through Methuselah, the message of mercy was extended for at least 969 years! And every day was a new opportunity for people to be saved. Therefore, the people of Noah's world were given 348,890 chances to repent.[4]

If we widen the lens even more, we can see God's gracious offer of salvation was demonstrated in multiple other ways to a global population whose wickedness was so great that "every intent of the thoughts of [their hearts] was only evil continually" (Genesis 6:5). Here's what God did:

1. The ark's door was a perpetual picture of salvation for the estimated billions of people who lived in Noah's day. An open door meant safe passage and deliverance was still accessible.

2. This preflood world would likely have been aware of the promise of a Savior (Genesis 3:15). Adam, Seth, and Enoch were all alive during some of Noah's generation, and Noah's lineage can be traced to Adam (Genesis 5:1-32).

3. God had already provided the example of a blood sacrifice for their ancestors' sin while in the garden (Genesis 3:21).

4. There was the "mark" on Cain, which not only protected him, but, along with his vagrant wandering, also reminded people of the consequences of sin (Genesis 4:12, 15; see also Romans 3:23; 6:23).

5. The fact that people died during this time was evidence that

the curse of sin was real and that they were a part of a sinful, fallen race (Genesis 2:17; 3:19).

6. The Bible also describes Enoch (Methuselah's father) as a prophetic preacher whose messages foretold of future judgment at the second coming of Christ (Jude 14-15).

7. The name of Enoch's son, Methuselah, was an almost-century-long sermon-warning, proclaimed every time he showed up or his name was mentioned.

8. The sudden rapture of Enoch would have been a visual sign to many that judgment was coming, since this appears to have been the core message of his ministry (Genesis 5:22-24).

9. Noah's own preaching gave people no excuse not to repent, and the building of the ark itself was the largest object lesson in human history, warning Earth's inhabitants of what was coming (1 Peter 3:19-20; 2 Peter 2:5).

10. Scripture tells us that embedded within the mind and conscience of every human is the knowledge of God's divine character and existence. Denying this fact requires willful suppression and results in wrath and judgment (Romans 1:18-21; 2:14-16).

So the notion that Noah's generation was somehow ignorant of their own sin or of the way of salvation cannot be supported through Scripture. To the contrary, the evidence strongly suggests that for 1,656 years, they were exposed in multiple ways to God's plan of salvation.[5] However, consumed by self and sin, they instead chose to ignore or dismiss it. According to Jesus, they filled their lives with "eating and drinking, marrying and giving in marriage, until the day that Noah entered the ark, and they did not understand [that is, realize the severity and reality] until the flood came and took them all away" (Matthew 24:38-39).

They had heard. They knew. They just didn't care. They squandered the opportunity.

Every single one of them.

And they missed the boat—literally. On the other hand, Noah took full advantage of his moment, all the way up to the time he and his family entered the ark.

Back to Us

Historically, believers in Christ have enjoyed 2,000 years' worth of opportunities to be salt and light in our world. But we currently find ourselves in a strange and unique moment in time—an hour that is perilous and prophetic, but also providential. As we saw in the previous chapter, our world will almost certainly face future pandemics, as well as a host of political, cultural, moral, economic, and military crises in the days to come. This is the nature and pattern of a fallen planet.

While most might conclude from such events that everything is falling apart, according to Scripture, it's actually falling *into place*. The Bible reminds us that as we look ahead at even worse times (the tribulation), God is still on His throne (Revelation 4:1-11) and no purpose of His can ever be thwarted (Job 42:2). This was a truth King Nebuchadnezzar learned the hard way, later confessing, "He does according to His will in the host of heaven and among the inhabitants of earth; and no one can ward off His hand or say to Him, 'What have you done?'" (Daniel 4:35).

Revelation tells us that what God has in store for planet Earth are things that "must take place" (Revelation 4:1). We can't simply ignore or wish away the challenging times ahead. And we certainly cannot speak them into nonexistence, as apostate preacher Kenneth Copeland claimed he would do with the COVID-19 virus.[6]

It is understandable that people are wondering whether life will ever be normal again. But what if that's not the case? What if our world situation becomes even more perilous and challenging? What does that mean for us? What kind of mindset should we adopt? How can we seize the day for Christ and continue moving forward?

The answer is found in open doors—doors of opportunity.

Consider for a moment that during the most acute days of the 2020 pandemic, CEO Jeff Bezos braced Amazon for what was projected to be a $1.5 billion loss in that year's second quarter. Instead, after making some adjustments, Amazon raised its net profits to $5.2 billion![7] Others also saw dramatic profits and successes in the worst months of the pandemic and lockdowns, including…

- videogame companies
- Clorox (disinfectant wipes)
- Peloton (revenue grew 66 percent in one quarter)
- Grocery chains like Publix ($1 billion increase) and Kroger (30 percent increase)
- 3M (maker of masks)
- Slack and Zoom videoconferencing companies (80 percent increase and a stock increase of 120 percent)[8]

Whether by default, happy accident, or visionary design, these companies capitalized on the crisis, the proof being in the profits.

Where others see obstacles, we must see open doors.

Opportunities to Thrive

The bride of Christ must do the same, only in a spiritual sense, viewing the challenges before us as opportunities to thrive and spread the name of Jesus across the street and the world. Where others see obstacles, we must see open doors. Instead of wondering "How are we going to make it?," we should ask, "How can I capture this moment for the glory of God?"

I see three doors wide open right now and begging us to pass through them. All three represent golden opportunities for those who belong to Jesus Christ. They are

- a door to biblical discernment
- a door to personal awakening
- a door to engage culture with the gospel

A Door of Biblical Discernment

As we continue to witness stage-setting prophecies developing before our eyes, we must also develop the ability to "understand the times, with knowledge of what [we] should do" (1 Chronicles 12:32). It was this very ability to understand and navigate life that characterized Paul's most passionate prayers for the Philippians: "This I pray, that your love may abound still more and more in real knowledge and all discernment" (1:9). He prayed essentially the same for the Colossians (1:9).

In an age of unlimited information via the internet, the masses of humanity nevertheless remain largely ignorant, unaware of past history and present happenings across their world. As far back as 2008, the Intercollegiate Studies Institute found that 71 percent of Americans of all backgrounds, incomes, and education failed a basic literacy test. Only 27 percent know that the Bill of Rights prohibits the establishment of an official religion in the United States.[9] A 2017 poll found that 37 percent cannot name a single right protected by the First Amendment. Some universities are considering abolishing their history departments, so low is the interest in the subject. At the same time, more Americans can "identify Michael Jackson as the composer of 'Beat It' and 'Billy Jean' than could identify the Bill of Rights as a body of Amendments to the Constitution."[10] The same survey found that "more than a third did not know the century in which the American Revolution took place."[11]

From 1964–2010, the number of Western civilization survey courses in America's colleges have declined to the point of near extinction.[12] Apparently the study of history is becoming history itself! Today's generation seems to have become experts at snapping selfies and posting on social media while simultaneously remaining largely uninformed about the course of their own civilization or the basics of the Bible, as shown by a Barna Group poll that found 12 percent of Americans think Joan of Arc was Noah's wife. A further survey revealed that more than 50 percent of graduating high school seniors thought Sodom and Gomorrah were husband and wife![13] That would be funny if it weren't true.

As for Christians and their grasp of the Bible, things aren't much better. Only 3 percent of teenagers who own a Bible read it daily. Among churchgoing adults, 19 percent read it daily, with 14 percent opening it once a week and 18 percent never reading it at all. In America, more than half of those who profess to be Christians believe their good works will help them get to heaven.[14] This is no surprise, given the statistics above about Bible reading.

Is it any wonder, then, that professing believers today not only fail to discern how the events of our world fit seamlessly into Bible prophecy, but also struggle to cope in an ever-increasingly godless culture?

The solution to this malady is for professing Christians to get back to, and *into*, the Bible, both personally and corporately. Jesus severely rebuked the churches at Pergamum and Thyatira for ignoring and dishonoring His Word by holding to wrong teaching and immorality (Revelation 2:14-16, 20). It is imperative that we who are Christians develop discernment concerning this prophetic season in which we find ourselves. At no other time in the past 2,000 years has it been more essential for the church to know where she is on God's prophetic timetable.

Therefore, we must return to the Word of God—reading, studying, discussing, and hearing it regularly. For when the Bible speaks, God speaks. And in these days, we *desperately* need to hear from God.

Put plainly, it's time for you to dive into the Word. And pastors must "work hard at preaching and teaching" the Word (1 Timothy 5:17). I encourage you to read books by respected authors on biblical topics related to sound doctrine and Bible prophecy. For unless we walk through this door of discernment, we will be caught up with the rest of the masses in a free-flowing river of ignorance, confusion, and anxiety.

A Door of Awakening

Many today pray for, speak of, and even prophesy about a coming great revival in the end times. And, to be fair, it is possible there may be some sort of global spiritual harvest in the days leading up to the rapture. However, as stated earlier, we see no such revival prophesied in Scripture. Instead, what we see foretold is a great falling away from the faith (1 Timothy 4:1; 2 Timothy 3:1; 2 Thessalonians 2:3).

But let's assume for a moment there *could* be an end-times awakening. If so, wouldn't it make sense for such a revival to begin with us as individuals? And for that to happen, we must wake up, purify and prepare our hearts, and protect ourselves from Satan's attacks and influence.

In fact, this was precisely Jesus' stern command to the church at Sardis: to "wake up" (Revelation 3:2; cf. Romans 13:11-12). It is not uncommon for both churches and believers to spiritually slumber in the midst of lives filled with Christian activity and service. Therefore, we must place ourselves under Scripture's searchlight, allowing God to do a daily "heart MRI" on us, which is what being exposed to the Word does (Hebrews 4:12). Doing this effectively "caffeinates" our souls, keeping us in touch with God and in tune with His desires for us.

> An ongoing awareness of Christ's return motivates us to be a pure bride who is ready to meet her beloved Bridegroom.

A second step in this personal revival process is maintaining our purity as we look forward to Christ's return. In 1 John 3:2-3, we read that the hope we have as we anticipate the rapture is a purifying hope—"everyone who has this hope fixed on Him purifies himself" (see also 2 Corinthians 7:1; 2 Peter 3:11-12). An ongoing awareness of Christ's return motivates us to be a pure bride who is ready to meet her beloved Bridegroom.

You want Him to find you ready, right?

That's one reason why Paul called the rapture "the blessed hope" (Titus 2:13). As we saw in chapter 8, the early church eagerly awaited Christ's coming and was anxious for their deliverance from this world and the wrath to come (1 Corinthians 1:7; Hebrews 9:28; 1 Thessalonians 1:10; 5:9; Jude 21). They even adopted an Aramaic word, *Maranatha*, meaning "our Lord—come!" to express to one another this spirit of expectation when they gathered (1 Corinthians 16:22). This anticipatory spirit is in response to the biblical doctrine of imminence—the teaching that His return is inevitable, next to occur, and could happen at any time.

In Mark 13:32-37, Jesus warned Jewish believers suffering in the future tribulation to pay attention and to "Be on the alert!"

concerning His second coming. He then listed specific signs that would precede His return at the close of the tribulation (Matthew 24:4-35), instructing them to be like a "doorkeeper" watching for these things (Mark 13:34). While the second coming will be preceded by seven years full of signs, the rapture contains no such prophesied pre-events or warning signs. And yet, in the absence of specific signs, the early church was still filled with expectation for the rapture. If Jesus was concerned those Jewish tribulation believers would be unprepared for an event that is preceded by multiple, visible, supernatural signs, how much more do we as Christians today need to be awake, alert, and anticipating the sign-less event of the rapture?

As believers living in the last days, we mustn't look for signs, but rather, for "the blessed hope" itself.

A Door to Engaging Culture

A third unique open-door opportunity we have in these last days is to infiltrate culture with our presence and the gospel message. On the night before His crucifixion, Jesus prayed for you, petitioning the Father not to take you out of the world, but instead, to keep you from the evil one (John 17:15). Three verses later, He dialed it up a notch by praying, "As You sent Me into the world, I also have *sent them* into the world" (verse 18; cf. 20:21). While this prayer was stated on behalf of the disciples, Jesus made it very clear that you and I are also in view in His prayer: "I do not ask on behalf of these alone, but for those also who believe in Me through their word" (verse 20).

May I ask you a simple question before we continue? Do you see yourself as a "sent one"? Is that how you view your relationship with your Lord? At the heart of Christ's commission to us is the fact that He has divinely called us to *be* His witnesses, not merely to *do* witnessing (Acts 1:8). His command to "go therefore and make disciples of all the nations" was given to us in the context of our everyday lives ("go" = "in your goings").

Our influence for Jesus must first be a natural and genuine overflow of our relationship with Him and our growth in His Word. We cannot be His witnesses if our lives contradict His message.

Think of this: The vast majority of unbelievers will never read a Bible or attend a church. But they will read *you*. In fact, they already have. You are Jesus' hands, feet, and voice in your culture. You are His light in the darkness (Matthew 5:14-16). His representative (John 17:18; 20:21). His royal ambassador, representing the King of kings in a foreign land (2 Corinthians 5:20). You are not responsible for how people react to God's truth and the message of the cross. In fact, you must expect that some will sneer, while others will want to hear more, with some even coming to belief (Acts 17:32-34). Your message, and even your very presence, will be an aroma of death to some, while to others it will be the fragrance of life itself (2 Corinthians 2:16).

> We have an abundance of ways to engage others regarding truth, life, crises, the future, salvation, and eternity.

To effectively represent Christ, we must continue being in the world while at the same time guarding ourselves from its pervasive influences and values (John 17:14-16, 18). We must learn how to *insulate* ourselves without *isolating* ourselves. This means we don't surround ourselves only with believers 24/7, but instead, using the knowledge and discernment found in Scripture, we strategically place ourselves in cultural circles and situations where we can have maximum influence for our Savior.

A door to biblical discernment.

A door to awakening.

A door to engaging culture.

Each of these passageways represents once-in-a-lifetime opportunities. What's more, the doors open to us are many. We have an abundance of ways to engage others regarding truth, life, crises, the future, salvation, and eternity. But time goes quickly and doors close unexpectedly. And the moment passes.

The Time Is Now

The prophetic clock is ticking. We cannot afford to miss God's open doors, as they will not always be available to us. Time is not on our side; therefore, we must embrace a sense of urgency in our mission.

This is *your* time. *Your* chance. *Your* opportunity. And *your* choice.

Now is the time to be His witness. *Now* is the time to serve the saints. *Now* is the time to do ministry. *Now* is the time to penetrate culture. The time is now to wake up and speak out. Don't be deceived—this moment of opportunity *will* pass. What will you do with it? What will you do with the time you have left? How will you manage your life and navigate the coming seasons of crisis? How will you, by God's grace and wisdom, take advantage of the opportunities staring you in the face? How will you use your stewardship for His gospel and glory?

I pray this book has triggered something inside you—something deep beneath the surface, producing a righteous rumbling in your spirit, one that will produce spiritual aftershocks long after you are gone and even into eternity.

Earlier on the morning of John F. Kennedy's final encounter with Billy Graham at the National Prayer Breakfast, the president gave a short three-minute speech. At its conclusion, he read a quote from Reverend Philip Brooks, a nineteenth-century clergyman in Boston:

"Do not pray for easy lives. Pray to be stronger men. Do not pray for tasks equal to your powers. Pray for powers equal to your tasks."[15]

I won't lie. The task before you is a formidable one. And you simply cannot allow your life to be an "irrecoverable moment." At times, your mission may seem insurmountable. But as you enter this era of global crisis, yet another door opens, one allowing you to see God's inexhaustible, glorious power working through you.

And when your life here on Earth comes to an end, it won't be so much the length of your days that will have defined you. Rather, like Methuselah, it will be the meaning of the name given to you by your Father. A name you bear with honor and reverence. A name infused with truth, confidence, and hope.

That name is *Christian*.

NOTES

Restless Planet

1. The most "famous" earthquake in US history to date is the 1906 San Francisco quake, which killed more than 3,000 people and left the city in ruins. It measured 7.8 on the Richter scale. "Remembering The 1964 Great Alaska Earthquake, the largest in U.S. history," *Washington Post*, March 27, 2014, https://www.washingtonpost.com/news/post-nation/wp/2014/03/27/remembering-the-1964-great-alaska-earthquake-the-largest-in-u-s-history/.

2. "1964 Alaska Earthquake," *History.com*, March 6, 2018, https://www.history.com/topics/natural-disasters-and-environment/1964-alaska-earthquake.

3. Thomas M. Brocher, et al, "The 1964 Great Alaska Earthquake and Tsunamis—A Modern Perspective and Enduring Legacies," March 4, 2014, https://pubs.usgs.gov/fs/2014/3018/.

Chapter 1—The Great Revealer

1. "Chinese Scientist Says Covid Came from Government Lab in Wuhan: Report," *ndtv.com*, Updated September 15, 2020, https://www.ndtv.com/world-news/chinese-virologist-li-meng-yan-claims-coronavirus-was-made-in-wuhan-lab-report-2295323

2. Faith Karimi and Maggie Fox, "George Floyd tested positive for coronavirus, but it had nothing to do with his death, autopsy shows," CNN, June 4, 2020, https://www.cnn.com/2020/06/04/health/george-floyd-coronavirus-autopsy/index.html.

3. Bill Hutchinson, "Police Officers Killed Surge 28% This Year," *ABC News*, July 22, 2020, https://abcnews.go.com/US/police-officers-killed-surge-28-year-point-civil/story?id=71773405.

4. Caitlin Dickerson, "'Please, I Don't Have Insurance' Businesses Plead with Protestors," *The New York Times*, May 31, 2020, https://www.nytimes.com/2020/05/31/us/minneapolis-protests-business-looting.html.

Chapter 2—Globalism at the Gates

1. This occurred during the reign of King Hezekiah and was the direct result of his prayer and Isaiah's prophecy (2 Kings 19:1-7, 15-37).

2. 1 Samuel 5:6-12; 1 Chronicles 21:1-17; Mark Hitchcock, *Corona Crisis: Plagues, Pandemics, and the Coming Apocalypse* (Nashville, TN: Thomas Nelson, 2020), 36.

3. Hitchcock, *Corona Crisis*, 36.

4. COVID-19 Coronavirus Pandemic, *worldometer*, October 12, 2020, https://www.worldometers.info/coronavirus/?fbclid=IwAR25TREd9T9_MmeKlfhUa-tZ3ay_JnL6zl7Wy I6g8GGuUhBhW1gQfwXvOoQ#countries.

5. Richard Partington, "WTO reports big slump in global trade as coronavirus takes toll," *The Guardian*, May 20, 2020, https://www.theguardian.com/business/2020/may/20/wto-reports-big-slump-in-global-trade-as-coronavirus-takes-toll.

6. Bryan Walsh, "The coronavirus is a force for deglobalization," *Axios*, May 20, 2020, https://www.axios.com/coronavirus-economic-globalization-744b0660-ce56-4ffa-93e9-cc4c20ee135c.html.

7. Ban Ki-moon, "I Was the Secretary-General of the U.N. Here's How the Coronavirus Can Bring the World Together," *Time*, April 15, 2020, https://time.com/collection-post/5820650/ban-ki-moon-global-relations-coronavirus/.

8. Ban Ki-moon, "I Was the Secretary General of the U.N."

9. *The Elders*, https://www.theelders.org.

10. *The Elders*, https://www.theelders.org.

11. Mia Hunt, "Ex-UK PM Gordon Brown calls for global government to tackle coronavirus pandemic, *Global Government Forum*, March 27, 2020, https://www.globalgovernmentforum.com/ex-uk-pm-gordon-brown-calls-for-global-government-to-tackle-coronavirus-pandemic/.

12. Mark Coeckelbergh, "Coronavirus and the need for global governance," *Democracy Without Borders*, April 8, 2020, https://www.democracywithoutborders.org/13204/coronavirus-and-the-need-for-global-governance/.

13. Coeckelbergh, "Coronavirus and the need for global governance."

14. Justin Haskins, "Introducing the 'Great Reset,' world leaders' radical plan to transform the economy," MSN, June 25, 2020, https://www.msn.com/en-us/news/politics/introducing-the-great-reset-world-leaders-radical-plan-to-transform-the-economy/ar-BB15XGsU.

15. Haskins, "Introducing the 'Great Reset.'"

16. Arnol Mehra, "The Great Reset after COVID-19 must put people first," *World Economic Forum*, June 23, 2020, https://www.weforum.org/agenda/2020/06/covid19-reset-people-first-inequality/.

17. Two other power blocs are present during the tribulation: a southern and northern coalition made up of Russia, North Africa, and Muslim nations of the Middle East (Daniel 11:40-41; Ezekiel 38), and an Eastern alliance made up of "the kings from the east" (Revelation 16:12). The first will be destroyed in the Gog-Magog War (Ezekiel 38–39), which will likely take place just after the rapture and around the beginning of the tribulation. The kings of the east will make their way to Armageddon, either to confront Antichrist and his armies, or to join them in an attempt to destroy Jerusalem and wage war against Jesus Christ.

18. "The Woman Riding the Beast," *laymanswatch*, http://laymanswatch.com/LaymansWatch_files/Misc/WomanAndTheBeast.htm.

19. Typically when John uses symbolism as it relates to a geographic location, he lets us know, as in Revelation 11:8, where Jerusalem "mystically is called Sodom and Egypt."

20. Tim LaHaye and Ed Hindson, *The Popular Encyclopedia of Bible Prophecy* (Eugene, OR: Harvest House, 2004), 42.

21. Mark Hitchcock, *The Amazing Claims of Bible Prophecy* (Eugene, OR: Harvest House, 2010), 117.

22. "Explaining the Treaty of Lisbon," *Europa*, December 1, 2009, https://ec.europa.eu/commission/presscorner/detail/en/MEMO_09_531.

Chapter 3—Caesar and God

1. Richard Nordquist, "What Is Doublespeak?," *ThoughtCo.*, April 2, 2018, https://www
.thoughtco.com/doublespeak-language-term-1690475.

2. *Shout Your Abortion*, https://shoutyourabortion.com/events/.

3. "Supreme Court of the United States: Obergefell et. Al v. Hodges, Director, Ohio
Department of Health, et al.," https://www.supremecourt.gov/opinions/14pdf/14-556
_3204.pdf.

4. California Family Council, "Good News: Penalizing 'Misgendering' with Hefty Fine
and/or Jail Time being Legally Challenged," *California Family Council*, February 27,
2018, https://californiafamily.org/2018/good-news-law-penalizing-misgendering-with
-hefty-fine-and-or-jail-time-being-legally-challenged/.

5. During the height of the COVID lockdown, among the world's most tightly controlled
countries were Cuba, China, Libya, Saudi Arabia, North Korea, and Syria. The vast
majority of oppressive regimes are Muslim countries in which free and fair elections do
not exist.

6. Timothy Snowball, "Avoiding government overreach in the COVID-19 recovery," *Pacific
Legal Foundation*, May 14, 2020, https://pacificlegal.org/avoiding-government-overreach
-in-the-covid-19-recovery/.

7. Snowball, "Avoiding government overreach in the COVID-19 recovery."

8. Mario Lotmore, "DOH admits inflated COVID-19 death numbers," *Lynnwood Times*,
May 21, 2020, https://lynnwoodtimes.com/2020/05/21/doh-admits-inflated-covid
-19-death-numbers/.

9. Jeff Deist, "Does the Coronavirus Make the Case for World Government?," *Mises Institute*, February 26, 2020, https://mises.org/power-market/does-coronavirus-make-case
-world-government.

10. Katie Keith, "Religious, Moral Exemptions From Contraceptive Coverage Mandates:
Second Verse, Same As The First," Health Affairs, November 9, 2018, https://www
.healthaffairs.org/do/10.1377/hblog20181109.87594/full/.

11. Utah Rep. Merrill Nelson, "10 terrifying examples of federal overreach," *Convention of
States Action*, May 22, 2019, https://conventionofstates.com/news/10-terrifying
-examples-of-federal-overreach.

12. Elizabeth Dias, "Conservative Christians See 'Seismic Implications' in Supreme Court
Ruling," *The New York Times*, June 15, 2020, https://www.nytimes.com/2020/06/15/us/
lgbtq-supreme-court-religious-freedom.html.

13. Dias, "Conservative Christians See 'Seismic Implications' in Supreme Court Ruling."

14. Wesley J. Smith, "Normalizing Pedophilia 2, *National Review*, August 27, 2013, https://
www.nationalreview.com/human-exceptionalism/normalizing-pedophilia-2-wesley
-j-smith/.

15. Michael Brown, "Normalizing 'Throuples' as We Mindlessly Careen Our Way
Down the Slippery Slope," *The Stream*, February 17, 2020, https://stream.org/
normalizing-throuples-as-we-mindlessly-careen-our-way-down-the-slippery-slope/.

16. "The Men Who Call Themselves Non-Offending Pedophiles," *Vice News*, https://www
.vice.com/en_us/article/j5y8zy/the-men-who-call-themselves-non-offending-pedophiles.

17. J. Paul Federoff, "The Pedophilia and Orientaton Debate and Its Implication for

Forensic Psychiatry," The Journal of the American Academy of Psychiatry and the Law, *AAPL*, June 2020, http://jaapl.org/content/48/2/146.

18. Campbell Robertson and Elizabeth Dias, "United Methodist Church Announces Plan to Split Over Same-Sex Marriage," *The New York Times*, January 3, 2020, https://www.nytimes.com/2020/01/03/us/methodist-split-gay-marriage.html.

19. Tom Gjelten, "Some See Plot to Create 'World Government' in Coronavirus Restrictions," *NPR*, May 8, 2020, https://www.npr.org/sections/coronavirus-live-updates/2020/05/08/853110793/some-see-plot-to-create-world-government-in-coronavirus-restrictions.

20. "Appeal," *Veritas liberabit vos.*, May 7, 2020, https://veritasliberabitvos.info/appeal/.

21. "Appeal."

22. Gjelten, "Some See Plot to Create 'World Government' in Coronavirus Restrictions."

23. Government is also a stewardship from God. And God's Word has something to say to the nations, kings, rulers, and judges who would take counsel against Him and His Word (Psalm 2). When governments stand for, tolerate, promote, and even legislate toward immorality and godlessness, then they have declared war on God. But He who sits in the heavens laughs at them.

24. See also Proverbs 24:21; Jeremiah 29:4-14; Matthew 22:21; 1 Timothy 2:1; Hebrews 10:32-34.

25. Adapted from dialogue that appears in Evan Andrews, "Patrick Henry's 'Liberty or Death' Speech," *History.com*, August 22, 2018, https://www.history.com/news/patrick-henrys-liberty-or-death-speech-240-years-ago.

26. "Nearly 1 million Christians reportedly martyred for their faith in last decade," *Fox News*, updated July 6, 2017, https://www.foxnews.com/world/nearly-1-million-christians-reportedly-martyred-for-their-faith-in-last-decade.

27. For more about America's Christian roots, see Jeff Kinley, *The End of America?* (Eugene, OR: Harvest House, 2017).

28. "#103: Polycarp's Martyrdom," *Christian History Institute*, https://christianhistoryinstitute.org/study/module/polycarp/.

Chapter 4—Technology and Satan's Superman

1. John Detrixhe, "Cashless payments are growing faster in India than just about anywhere else," *QZ*, November 12, 2019, https://qz.com/india/1746910/cashless-payments-growing-faster-in-india-than-almost-anywhere-else/.

2. James Booth, "A look into the future: How COVID-19 changed payments," *Retail Dive*, June 18, 2020, https://www.retaildive.com/spons/a-look-into-the-future-how-covid-19-changed-payments/579301/.

3. Shawn M. Carter, "Cash is still king in the United States—but for how much longer?," *Fox Business*, October 18, 2019, https://www.foxbusiness.com/money/cash-is-still-king-in-the-united-states-but-for-how-much-longer

4. Sulabh Agarwal, "The Top Eight Ways COVID-19 Will Impact Payments," *Accenture*, April 27, 2020, https://bankingblog.accenture.com/top-eight-ways-covid-19-will-impact-payments

5. Luana Pascu, "Biometric facial recognition hardware present in 90% of smartphones by

2024," *Biometric Update.com*, January 7, 2020, https://www.biometricupdate.com/202001/biometric-facial-recognition-hardware-present-in-90-of-smartphones-by-2024.

6. Daniel Keyes, "Amazon is developing a terminal that lets consumers scan their hand to check out," *Business Insider*, January 22, 2020, https://www.businessinsider.com/amazon-developing-biometric-payment-terminal-2020-1.

7. "Can Amazon Give Biometric Payments A Hand—In The Store?," *PYMNTS*, September 5, 2019, https://www.pymnts.com/amazon/2019/amazon-gives-biometric-payments-a-hand-in-the-store/.

8. "Why Amazon And Other Retailers Are Turning To Biometrics," PYMNTS, January 27, 2020, https://www.pymnts.com/news/retail/2020/why-amazon-and-other-retailers-are-turning-to-biometrics/.

9. Lauren Debter, "The Race To Bring Cashierless Checkout To Stores Heats Up With Giant Eagle Debut," *Forbes*, September 1, 2020, https://www.forbes.com/sites/lauren debter/2020/09/01/grabango-cashierless-checkout-giant-eagle-getgo-debut/#16902863ab55.

10. It appears that Satan even appoints specific demons in charge of regions and nations (see Daniel 10:13).

11. "The Harbinger 39: Satan's DNA and the Antichrist," *Issuu*, June 19, 2012, https://issuu.com/audioactivated/docs/the_harbinger_39.

12. Justine Morrow, "Smart Tattoo Technology: The Future Within Skin," *Tattoodo*, https://www.tattoodo.com/a/smart-tattoo-technology-the-future-within-skin-14567.

13. Morrow, "Smart Tattoo Technology: The Future Within Skin."

Chapter 5—The End-Times Economic Collapse

1. The United Nations recognizes 251 countries and territories, while the United States recognizes only 195. Matt Rosenberg, "The Number of Countries in the World," *ThoughtCo.*, updated February 27, 2020, https://www.thoughtco.com/number-of-countries-in-the-world-1433445.

2. Madeleine Ngo, "Small Businesses Are Dying by the Thousands, and No One Is Tracking the Carnage," *Bloomberg*, August 11, 2020, https://www.bloomberg.com/news/articles/2020-08-11/small-firms-die-quietly-leaving-thousands-of-failures-uncounted.

3. Bureau of Labor Statistics, "News Release," *BLS*, May 8, 2020, https://www.bls.gov/news.release/archives/empsit_05082020.pdf.

4. Gita Gopinath, "The Great Lockdown: Worst Economic Downturn Since the Great Depression," *IMFBlog*, April 14, 2020, https://blogs.imf.org/2020/04/14/the-great-lockdown-worst-economic-downturn-since-the-great-depression/.

5. Alexis C. Madrigal and Robinson Meyer, "How Could the CDC Make That Mistake?," *The Atlantic*, May 21, 2020, https://www.theatlantic.com/health/archive/2020/05/cdc-and-states-are-misreporting-covid-19-test-data-pennsylvania-georgia-texas/611935/.

6. "Global Economic Effects of COVID-19," *Congressional Research Service*, September 21, 2020, https://fas.org/sgp/crs/row/R46270.pdf.

7. "What are Black Swan events?," *Black Swan*, http://blackswanevents.org/?page_id=26.

8. "Global Risks 2018: Fractures, Fears and Failures," *World Economic Forum*, https://reports.weforum.org/global-risks-2018/global-risks-2018-fractures-fears-and-failures/.

9. Mark Hitchcock, *The End: The Complete Overview of Bible Prophecy and the End of Days* (Carol Stream, IL: Tyndale House Publishers, 2012), 280-281.

10. David Jeremiah, *Escape the Coming Night* (Dallas, TX: Word, 1990), 96.

11. Zack Beauchamp, "The New York Times' first article about Hitler's rise is absolutely stunning," *Vox*, updated March 3, 2016, https://www.vox.com/2015/2/11/8016017/ny-times-hitler.

12. "Barack Obama's Remarks in St. Paul," *The New York Times*, June 3, 2008, https://www.nytimes.com/2008/06/03/us/politics/03text-obama.html.

13. The Greek word here is *pyrrós*, referring to a fiery red color. From *pýr* ("fire").

14. Soliloquies in England and Later Soliloquies (1922).

15. Both Mark and Luke include earthquakes between the war and famine prophesied in Revelation 6.

16. In AD 92, the Emperor Domitian ordered half the existing vineyards in Italy to be destroyed due to the shortage of wheat and overabundance of wine. The populace responded so volatilely that he was forced to rescind the order. Robert Thomas, *Revelation 1-7, An Exegetical Commentary* (Chicago, IL: Moody Publishers, 1992), 434.

17. Charles Swindoll, *Insights on Revelation* (Grand Rapids, MI: Zondervan, 2011), 111.

18. Based on a current world population of 7.8 billion. This number would change depending on how many are taken in the rapture.

19. "This is not the end of the world, according to Christians who study the end of the world," *The Washington Post*, March 17, 2020, https://www.washingtonpost.com/religion/2020/03/17/not-end-of-the-world-coronavirus-bible-prophecy/.

20. "Diseases That Can Spread Between Animals and People," *Centers for Disease Control and Prevention*, https://www.cdc.gov/healthypets/diseases/index.html.

21. Though estimates vary, many believe Earth's population at the time of Noah to conservatively be around 750,000,000. "What Was the Pre-Flood Population Like?," *Answers in Genesis*, January 6, 2016, https://answersingenesis.org/noahs-ark/pre-flood-population/.

Chapter 6—Israel and the Rise of Antisemitism

1. Michael Livingston, ed., "Siege of Jerusalem: Introduction," *University of Rochester Middle English Text Series*, https://d.lib.rochester.edu/teams/text/livingston-siege-of-jerusalem-introduction.

2. Olivier J. Melnick, *End-Times Antisemitism: A New Chapter in the Longest Hatred* (Tustin, CA: Hope for Today Publications, 2018), 68.

3. Melnick, *End-Times Antisemitism*.

4. Excerpt from *Luther's Works, Volume 47: The Christian in Society IV* (Philadelphia: Fortress Press, 1971), 268-293.

5. Melnick, *End-Times Antisemitism*, p. 48.

6. Hugh Fogelman, *Christianity Uncovered* (Bloomington, IN: Author House, 2012), 248.

7. C.N. Trueman, "Jews in Nazi Germany," *History Learning Site*, October 26, 2020, https://www.historylearningsite.co.uk/nazi-germany/jews-in-nazi-germany/.

8. "Document for May 14th: Press Release Announcing U.S. Recognition of Israel," *National Archives*, https://www.archives.gov/historical-docs/todays-doc/index.html?dod-date=514.

9. Also known as the Israeli War of Independence.

10. "Palestinians Want to Finish the Job that Hitler Started," *YouTube*, uploaded by Andrew Iniesta, December 3, 2011, https://www.youtube.com/watch?v=yWwyCgUFaJ0.

11. *ADL/Global 100*, https://global100.adl.org/map.

12. "Antisemitic Incidents Hit All-Time High in 2019," *Anti-Defamation League*, May 12, 2020, https://www.adl.org/news/press-releases/antisemitic-incidents-hit-all-time-high-in-2019.

13. Joshua Teitelbaum, "What Iranian Leaders Really Say About Doing Away with Israel," *Jewish Center for Public Affairs*, 2008, https://www.jcpa.org/text/ahmadinejad2-words.pdf.

14. Nigel Chiwaya, "Anti-Jewish Attacks Are Part of a Wave of 'More Violent' Hate Crimes," *NBC News*, January 3, 2020, https://www.nbcnews.com/news/us-news/anti-semitic-attacks-more-violent-hate-crimes-new-york-n1110036.

15. Jeffrey Goldberg, "Is It Time for the Jews to Leave Europe?," *The Atlantic*, April 2015, https://www.theatlantic.com/magazine/archive/2015/04/is-it-time-for-the-jews-to-leave-europe/386279/.

16. Toi Staff, "One In Five Brits Believe Antisemitic Virus Conspiracies," *The Times of Israel*, May 26, 2020, https://www.timesofisrael.com/one-in-five-brits-believe-anti-semitic-virus-conspiracies-survey/.

17. Donna Rachel Edmunds, "PA Blames Israel for Coronavirus Cases in West Bank," *The Jerusalem Post*, July 23, 2020, https://www.jpost.com/arab-israeli-conflict/pa-blames-israel-for-coronavirus-cases-in-west-bank-636009.

18. Stuart Winer, "Sheldon Adelson Is Puppet Master Pulling Trump-Pompeos Strings," *The Times of Israel*, June 21, 2020, https://www.timesofisrael.com/roger-waters-sheldon-adelson-puppet-master-pulling-trump-pompeos-strings/.

Chapter 7—Times of the Signs

1. See also similar warnings in Deuteronomy 4:2; 12:32; Proverbs 30:6; Jeremiah 26:2.

2. Shaun Walker, "Cult leader who claims to be reincarnation of Jesus arrested in Russia," *The Guardian*, September 22, 2020, https://www.theguardian.com/world/2020/sep/22/cult-leader-vissarion-reincarnation-jesus-arrested-siberia-russia.

3. "Vital Statistics: Jewish Population of the World: 1882-Present," *Jewish Virtual Library*, https://www.jewishvirtuallibrary.org/jewish-population-of-the-world. (This number represents roughly half of all Jews alive today.)

4. "PROPHECY WATCH: So many Jews are returning to Israel that the Govt. is concerned they won't be able to contain them," *End Times Headlines*, August 1 2020, https://endtimeheadlines.org/2020/08/prophecy-watch-so-many-jews-are-returning-to-israel-that-the-govt-is-concerned-they-wont-be-able-to-contain-them/?fbclid=IwAR0zp2z2xIJCMBE87V8jZ8-AFE-juIa5Aksg536kimb30q7M1NaAvfLemWQ.

5. *Global Citizen*, https://www.globalcitizen.org/en/connect/togetherathome/.

6. Lahav Harkov, "The Peace Treaties Between the UAE, Bahrain and Israel Are Signed,"

The Jerusalem Post, September 16, 2020, https://www.jpost.com/middle-east/israel-uae
-bahrain-sign-game-changing-normalization-deal-watch-live-642368.

7. Harkov, "The Peace Treaties."

8. *Temple Institute*, https://templeinstitute.org.

9. "The Red Heifer and the Third Temple in End-Time Prophecy," *The Messianic Prophecy
    Bible Project*, https://free.messianicbible.com/feature/the-red-heifer-and-the-third-tem
    -ple-in-end-time-prophecy/. See also Numbers 19:1-10.

10. Angie Chui, "Rob Bell Says Church Will Become Increasingly Irrelevant If It Holds to
    Words of the Bible on Marriage," *Christianity Today*, February 19, 2015, https://www
    .christiantoday.com/article/rob-bell-says-church-will-become-increasingly-irrelevant-if
    -it-holds-to-words-of-the-bible-on-marriage/48377.htm.

11. Lindy Lowry, "Christian Persecution by the Numbers," *Open Doors*, January 16, 2019,
    https://www.opendoorsusa.org/christian-persecution/stories/christian-persecution-by
    -the-numbers/.

12. Lowry, "Christian Persecution by the Numbers."

13. Elana Schor, "Pastor of Mega-church Arrested for Holding Two Sunday Services with
    Hundreds of People," *Click 2 Houston*, March 30, 2020, https://www.click2houston
    .com/news/2020/03/30/florida-officials-seek-arrest-for-pastor-that-violated-rules/.

14. Anugrah Kumar, "Pastor John MacArthur May Face Fine, Arrest for Holding Indoor
    Services: 'We will obey God rather than men,'" *Christian Post*, August 3, 2020, https://
    www.christianpost.com/news/pastor-john-macarthur-may-face-fine-arrest-for-holding
    -indoor-services-we-will-obey-god-rather-than-men.html.

15. "The Christ Quake," *Evidence for God from Science*, November 10, 2013, http://discus
    sions.godandscience.org/viewtopic.php?t=38866.

Chapter 8—The Coming Super Crisis

1. These estimates represent between 1 to 5.4 percent of the total population of the world at
    that time.

2. N.T. Wright, "Farewell to the Rapture," *NT Wright Online*, excerpted from *The Bible
    Review*, 2001, https://ntwrightpage.com/2016/07/12/farewell-to-the-rapture/.

3. Ed Hindson and Mark Hitchcock, *Can We Still Believe in the Rapture?* (Eugene, OR:
    Harvest House, 2017), 92-97.

4. Hindson and Hitchcock, *Can We Still Believe in the Rapture?*, 82-83.

5. *Theological Dictionary of the New Testament* (Grand Rapids, MI: William B. Eerdmans
    Publishing Company, 1985), s.v. *harpázo*.

6. Here are all the verses where *harpázo* is used in the New Testament, along with the mean-
    ing in each context: Matthew 11:12—take by force; Matthew 12:29—carry off; Mat-
    thew 13:19—snatches away; John 6:15—take by force; John 10:12—snatch by force; John
    10:29—snatch by force; Acts 8:39—snatch away, disappear; Acts 23:10—take away by
    force; 2 Corinthians 12:2—caught up to heaven; 2 Corinthians 12:4—caught up into
    Paradise; 1 Thessalonians 4:17—caught up…in the clouds; Jude 23—(quickly) snatching
    out of the fire; Revelation 12:5—(referring to Jesus) caught up to God (at the ascension).

7. This Greek word refers to "that which cannot be divided" or an "indivisible amount of
    time."

8. Matthew 5:13.

9. Romeo Vitelli, "Are We Facing a Post-Covid-19 Suicide Epidemic?," *Psychology Today*, June 7, 2020, https://www.psychologytoday.com/us/blog/media-spotlight/202006/ are-we-facing-post-covid-19-suicide-epidemic.

10. Stephanie Pappas, "What If 200 Million People Go Missing on Saturday?" *Live Science*, May 20, 2001, https://www.livescience.com/14251-200-million-rapture-12.html.

11. Erik Hayden, "Atheists Schedule May 21st 'Rapture Parties,'" *The Atlantic*, May 18, 2011, https://www.theatlantic.com/national/archive/2011/05/atheists-planning-rapture-party -may-21st/350840/.

12. "Table: Christian Population as Percentages of Total Population by Country," December 19, 2011, https://www.pewforum.org/2011/12/19/table-christian-population-as -percentages-of-total-population-by-country/.

13. "Child Population: Number of Children (In Millions) Ages 0–17 in the United States by Age, 1950–2019 and Projected 2020–2050," *Child Stats*, https://www.childstats.gov/ americaschildren/tables/pop1.asp.

14. Pappas, "What If 200 Million People Go Missing on Saturday?"

15. Pappas, "What If 200 Million People Go Missing on Saturday?"

16. Janet I. Tu, "Atheists counter prediction of doom with 'Rapture party,'" *The Seattle Times*, May 16, 2011, https://www.seattletimes.com/seattle-news/atheists-counter-prediction -of-doom-with-rapture-party/.

Chapter 9—Be Still and Know That I Am God

1. Katherine Ham, "Mental Health an Emerging Crisis of Covid Epidemic," *WebMD*, May 8, 2020, https://www.webmd.com/lung/news/20200508/mental-health-emerging -crisis-of-covid-pandemic.

2. R. Laird Harris, Gleason L. Archer Jr., Bruce K. Waltke, *Theological Wordbook of the Old Testament, Vol. 2* (Chicago,IL: Moody Press, 1980), 871.

3. See also Psalms 56:3; 55:1-8, 16-23; Isaiah 12:2; 43:1-5.

Chapter 10—Our Finest Hour

1. "Billy Graham," *Bible.org*, February 2, 2009, https://bible.org/illustration/billy-graham.

2. Bodie Hodge, "How Long Did It Take for Noah to Build the Ark?," *Answers in Genesis*, June 1, 2010, https://answersingenesis.org/bible-timeline/how-long-did-it-take-for-noah -to-build-the-ark/.

3. Arthur W. Pink, *Gleanings in Genesis* (Chicago: Moody Press, 1922), 88.

4. Calculated using the Jewish calendar of 360 days in a year multiplied by 969, the number of years Methuselah lived.

5. The flood occurred in 2348 B.C.—David Wright, "Timeline for the Flood," *Answers in Genesis*, March 9, 2012, https://answersingenesis.org/bible-timeline/timeline-for-the -flood/.

6. Alex Woodward, "Coronavirus: Televangelist Kenneth Copeland 'Blows Wind of God' at Covid-19 to 'Destroy' Pandemic," *Independent*, April 6, 2020, https://www .independent.co.uk/news/world/americas/kenneth-copeland-blow-coronavirus-pray -sermon-trump-televangelist-a9448561.html.

7. "Amazon.com Announces Second Quarter Results," *Amazon*, July 30, 2020, https://s2.q4cdn.com/299287126/files/doc_financials/2020/q2/Q2-2020-Amazon-Earnings-Release.pdf?ots=1&ascsubtag=%5b%5dvg%5be%5d21112409%5br%5dgoogle.com%5bt%5dw%5bd%5dD.

8. Jordan Valinsky, "Business Is Booming for These 14 Companies During the Coronavirus Pandemic," *The Mercury News*, May 7, 2020, https://www.mercurynews.com/2020/05/07/business-is-booming-for-these-14-companies-during-the-coronavirus-pandemic/.

9. "American's Increasing Ignorance of American History & Government Can No Longer Be Ignored," *American Heritage*, https://americanheritage.org/wp-content/uploads/2017/02/Americas-Increasing-Ignorance-Civic-Studies-Summaries.pdf.

10. Max Fisher, "Americans vs. Basic Historical Knowledge," *The Atlantic*, June 3, 2010, https://www.theatlantic.com/politics/archive/2010/06/americans-vs-basic-historical-knowledge/340761/.

11. Max Fisher, "Americans vs. Basic Historical Knowledge."

12. "American's Increasing Ignorance of American History & Government Can No Longer Be Ignored."

13. Albert Mohler, "The Scandal of Biblical Illiteracy: It's Our Problem," *AlbertMohler.com*, January 20, 2016, http://www.albertmohler.com/2016/01/20/the-scandal-of-biblical-illiteracy-its-our-problem-4/.

14. Leah MarieAnn Klett, "Over Half of US Christians Believe Good Works Will Get Them into Heaven: Study," *Christian Post*, August 11, 2020, https://www.christianpost.com/news/over-half-of-us-christians-believe-good-works-will-get-them-into-heaven-study.html.

15. "Remarks at the 11th Annual Presidential Prayer Breakfast, 7 February 1963," *JFKLibrary.org*, https://www.jfklibrary.org/asset-viewer/archives/JFKWHA/1963/JFKWHA-161-008/JFKWHA-161-008.

ABOUT THE AUTHOR

Jeff Kinley (ThM, Dallas Theological Seminary) has authored over 30 books and speaks across the country. His ministry equips churches to discern the times. Jeff's weekly *Vintage Truth* podcasts are heard in more than 80 countries. He and his wife live in Arkansas and have three grown sons.

You can connect with Jeff at jeffkinley.com.

OTHER GREAT HARVEST HOUSE BOOKS BY JEFF KINLEY

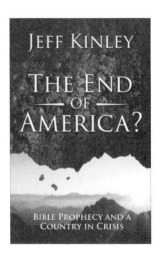

What happens when a country turns away from faith in God? Jeff Kinley explores historical and biblical precedents for the demise of a nation and offers valuable perspective on the future of America.

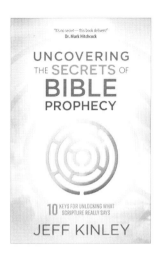

In this helpful, easy-to-read guide to understanding the nature and purpose of prophetic passages, Jeff Kinley will show you the five biggest mistakes people make in their studies, along with the major views and interpretive principles you need to know.

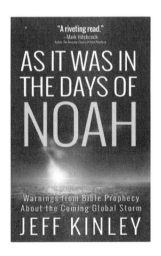

This powerful book explores the similarities between Noah's day and ours, such as the rapid rise in evil and increasingly flagrant disregard for God. A captivating read that affirms the urgency of living wisely and "redeeming the time" as we see the last days drawing nearer.

To learn more about Harvest House books and
to read sample chapters, visit our website:

www.harvesthousepublishers.com

HARVEST HOUSE PUBLISHERS
EUGENE, OREGON